Praise for

WAKING UP IN *Paris*

"Heartbroken Venus moves to Paris. Unflinchingly honest, entertaining, and real, *Waking Up in Paris* is an enlightened journey back to wholeness."

— **John Gray, Ph.D.**, #1 best-selling relationship author of all time

"In the deepest sense, life is a spiritual journey. In this incredibly heartfelt book, Sonia Choquette opens the gateway for you to accompany her and her daughter on her spiritual sojourn in Paris. Part *Under the Tuscan Sun*, part *Eat Pray Love,* and part journey of the heart. You'll laugh, you'll cry, and along the way you'll gain valuable life lessons. And for anyone who's starting over in life, you'll be inspired beyond measure. Highly recommended!"

— **Denise Linn**, best-selling author of *Energy Strands*

"Are you going through a dark time, or do you know people who are? This lyrical, uplifting, and life-changing book is for you and them. It is *not* filled with 'do this-do that' instructions that might pile on to an already daunting situation. Instead, it tells a story. An honest, 'I'll go first' story that will make you laugh, reflect, tear up, and open up to real-life ways to transform dark into light and recreate the quality of life you want, need, and deserve. Read it and reap!"

— **Sam Horn**, author of *Got Your Attention?*

"Never before have I come across a memoir with Paris as a spiritual teacher. Choquette expertly illustrates how when you heal internally, the external beauty is revealed. A simply wonderful read."

— **Janice MacLeod**, *New York Times* best-selling author of *Paris Letters* and *A Paris Year*

"*Waking Up in Paris* is about the ultimate pilgrimage we can dare to go on; it's about the humbling and humorous process we get initiated into when we want to find true love; it's about finally staying still, in order to heal, all the way back and all the way through. It's about coming home, at last, to this unlit cathedral that waits for us, in our own sacred hearts."

— **Meggan Watterson**, author of *Reveal* and *How to Love Yourself (and Sometimes Other People)*

WAKING UP IN
Paris

ALSO BY SONIA CHOQUETTE

Books/Oracle Cards

The Answer Is Simple . . .
Love Yourself, Live Your Spirit!

The Answer Is Simple Oracle Cards

Ask Your Guides: Connecting
to Your Divine Support System

Ask Your Guides Oracle Cards

Diary of a Psychic: Shattering the Myths

The Fool's Wisdom Oracle Cards

Grace, Guidance, and Gifts:
Sacred Blessings to Light Your Way

The Intuitive Spark: Bringing Intuition
Home to Your Child, Your Family, and You

Soul Lessons and Soul Purpose: A
Channeled Guide to Why You Are Here

Soul Lessons and
Soul Purpose Oracle Cards

The Time Has Come . . .
to Accept Your Intuitive Gifts!

Traveling at the Speed of Love

Trust Your Vibes at Work,
and Let Them Work for You

Trust Your Vibes Oracle Cards

Trust Your Vibes: Secret
Tools for Six-Sensory Living

Tune In: Let Your Intuition
Guide You to Fulfillment and Flow

Vitamins for the Soul: Daily Doses of
Wisdom for Personal Empowerment

Walking Home: A Pilgrimage
from Humbled to Healed

Your 3 Best Super Powers:
Meditation, Imagination & Intuition

CD Programs

Ask Your Guides: How to Connect
with Your Spiritual Support System
(6-CD and 4-CD sets)

Attunement to Higher Vibrational
Living, with Mark Stanton Welch
(4-CD set)

How to Trust Your Vibes at
Work, and Let Them Work for You
(4-CD set)

Meditations for Receiving Divine
Guidance, Support, and Healing
(2-CD set)

The Power of Your Spirit: Use It Now!
(4-CD set)

Trust Your Vibes: Secret Tools
for Six-Sensory Living (6-CD set)

All of the above are available at your local
bookstore, or may be ordered by visiting:

Hay House USA: www.hayhouse.com®
Hay House Australia: www.hayhouse.com.au
Hay House UK: www.hayhouse.co.uk
Hay House India: www.hayhouse.co.in

WAKING UP IN

Paris

Overcoming Darkness
in the City of Light

SONIA
CHOQUETTE

HAY HOUSE, INC.
Carlsbad, California • New York City
London • Sydney • Johannesburg
Vancouver • New Delhi

Published and distributed in the United States by: Hay House, Inc.: www
.hayhouse.com® • *Published and distributed in Australia by:* Hay House Australia Pty. Ltd.: www.hayhouse.com.au • *Published and distributed in the United
Kingdom by:* Hay House UK, Ltd.: www.hayhouse.co.uk • *Distributed in Canada by:* Raincoast Books: www.raincoast.com • *Published in India by:* Hay House
Publishers India: www.hayhouse.co.in

Cover design: Jenny Johnson • *Interior design:* Pamela Homan

Cataloging-in-Publication Data is on file at the Library of Congress

Hardcover ISBN: 978-1-4019-4446-9

10 9 8 7 6 5 4 3 2 1
1st edition, April 2018

Printed in the United States of America

I would like to dedicate this book to my
two beautiful daughters, Sonia and Sabrina
Choquette-Tully, who both stood by me in my hour
of darkness and walked with me back into the light.
I am so blessed to have you two gorgeous spirits as
my closest soul companions and sweetest friends in
life. And to the beautiful spirit that is Paris: You
woke me up to the deepest beauty in my soul
and helped me embrace the beauty in
all things and all experiences.

Contents

Part Three: THE OLD MAN

Part Four: THE SANCTUARY

Prologue

As a spiritual teacher and intuitive guide for the majority of my life, I have observed that most people are initially attracted to spirituality—whether to meditation, awakening intuition, or connecting to higher awareness—because they feel these practices will provide them with the strength to confront life's inevitable challenges and disappointments. They often hope that spirituality will serve as a cloak of invulnerability that will protect them against psychic pain.

In fact, the real benefit of spiritual awakening is that it allows us to embrace our vulnerability, to begin to disarm, to un-shield our sensitive hearts, and to boldly face and fully embrace everything that arises in life with arms wide-open. It is this stripping away of our ego defenses that allows for authentic connection to occur, first with ourselves, then with others.

Only when we are fully transparent and available to all that we experience and all that we feel, free of judgment, can we experience genuine self-love and self-compassion, or feel profound love and compassion for others. To live a truly guided spiritual life is to accept our fragility and the vicissitudes of being. It is to lean fully into the fire of life's challenges rather than fight against them. It means to be open to all that we encounter and not to run away and hide from it. To live this way takes courage, a word derived from the French word *cœur,* meaning "heart."

To live with a heart fully open means letting go of control and riding the wave of life's unfolding. It is messy and painful and even humiliating, but well worth it. At least it has been for me.

Part One

THE END

Falling Apart

This should have been a celebratory evening. I was about to speak to 1,000 people—one of my largest events ever as a spiritual teacher and writer. The topic was my newly released book, *Walking Home: A Pilgrimage from Humbled to Healed.* In the book, I recount my experience two years earlier of having dealt with the loss of two family members only six short weeks apart, followed by the sudden implosion of my 32-year marriage a month later, by going on an 800-kilometer spiritual pilgrimage across Spain, known as the Camino de Santiago.

The Camino is renowned the world over for its healing effects and its ability to transform loss and grief into acceptance and forgiveness, all of which, given my shattered inner state, I desperately needed. Under a mountain of grief and heartache that nearly suffocated me, I showed up to the Camino in pieces and began the greatest physical and spiritual healing journey of my life to date. Five weeks and a lifetime or more of introspection later, I completed my pilgrimage and returned home with a deep level of peace and acceptance in my heart that I had never known before. I wanted to share my experiences in the hopes that they would bring peace to others facing loss and grief as well.

Unfortunately, my own sense of peace was shattered again shortly after I returned from my healing journey . . .

When I returned from my pilgrimage 15 months earlier, it seemed as though the Camino de Santiago's healing reputation was indeed well earned: a month after I found my way back to Chicago, in August, my then-estranged husband, Patrick, contacted me and said he loved me and wanted to work on putting our marriage back together, which seemed like a miracle unto itself.

Surprised but overjoyed, I suggested that, as a way for us to heal as a couple, we walk the Camino together. Having just experienced its deeply transformative effect, I thought it could be a profoundly healing shared experience that would symbolically take us out of our troubled past and lead us into a cooperative and trusting future once and for all. He agreed and the future began to look fantastic—for me, for him, and for our family.

We planned our healing pilgrimage for the following June, 10 months from that meeting, and began a huge effort to try and understand one another and repair our connection in the meantime. He lived in Colorado and I lived in our home in Chicago at the time, so much of this took place long distance. It wasn't easy, but we were trying.

Knowing from experience what a rigorous journey the Camino would be, I also began to prepare for my second Camino pilgrimage.

Unlike the first time, when I waited until the very last minute to get ready, I put real thought into what lay ahead so I would be able to keep up with Patrick when we went together. He was athletic and I wasn't. I didn't want to hamper our healing pilgrimage by limping along the path as I had for much of my first journey. No, this time I would be strong and able. Instead of him running ahead and waiting impatiently for me to catch up, as had so often been the case over the years, we would walk side by side.

I bought new boots for the trip, as my old ones had destroyed my feet. I properly broke them in so there would be no complaining on my part. Knowing the importance of packing lightly (something I did not know or respect the first time I walked the Camino), I chose my clothes carefully and pared down to the minimum of basics. After all, I wanted this Camino to be one of leaving all excess baggage behind.

I was also acutely aware of how I much wanted to accommodate Patrick on this adventure instead of asking him to accommodate me, a trait I knew had caused a lot of stress and resentment in our marriage over the years. I worked out at the gym, lifting weights and doing squats *and bench presses so I would be strong and agile on the trip. I knew these things would help me keep up and were also important to Patrick.*

I booked my ticket and began to plan the logistics of the journey all over again, assuming that Patrick was making his own plans to meet me in Spain on June 1.

Imagine my shock when, just five weeks before we were to leave for Spain, I opened an e-mail from my ex-attorney informing me that Patrick was not calling off the divorce he had asked for, as he had said he was doing, but rather was putting it "on hold" until after our return. He would decide whether he wanted a divorce or not depending on how the Camino pilgrimage turned out.

My ego flipped out. I refused these conditions. In response, Patrick asked for a divorce. The pilgrimage was off.

Like a thunderbolt striking me in the back of my heart, it was done. He went to court. I sent my lawyer instead. I flew to Spain as planned and started my second pilgrimage, alone, more shocked and broken this time than the first.

The second pilgrimage, like the first one, took just over five weeks to complete. Only this time I didn't have any long, deep conversations with God along the way. Instead, I ignored God when I wasn't busy telling him how devastated and betrayed I felt.

I didn't go into churches and light candles and pray in gratitude. For the most part, I prayed to Mother Mary for help outside in the fields.

While I was running across Spain in a completely numb state, my now ex-husband came to the house and took all that was his from the settlement, including the gourmet kitchen stove. On his way out the door, he posted a lovely Facebook message for all who knew us to see: "Free at LAST."

Upon my return toward the end of July, I discovered that while I was away, the house had flooded and sewage had backed up into the basement from the floor drain under the carpet and sat there for almost the entire time I was gone. Since no one was in the house, no one discovered it.

I returned to find that the stench and mold from the sewage had overtaken the entire house and everything underground was rotting. It *was so symbolic of my inner world that I almost had to laugh but could only cry instead.*

How could this have happened so fast? Everything I had devoted the past 32 years to building was gone in a flash. The heart of our home was no longer beating, the foundation rotting to the core like a dead body left to decompose in the heat.

Thank God for my two grown daughters, Sonia and Sabrina. Both showed up to help tape our broken family together.

Just as I was washing my hands after throwing out the last bit of rotting carpet and destroyed furniture, my book came out. It seemed as if a lifetime had passed since I wrote it—how could I possibly relate to that heartened, hopeful person I was a mere 12 months earlier?

And now, here I was, late September, four months after the divorce and less than 100 miles from where Patrick was living in Colorado, invited to share the story of my epic healing journey across Spain with over 1,000 people, and instead of being filled with joy and excitement, my nervous system was completely frayed, my heart was destroyed, and I could barely open my mouth without bursting into tears.

Sonia had accompanied me to Denver. As soon as Sonia and Sabrina finished college, I enlisted them to accompany me to my events, as they helped me with the music and various logistics. This time, it was Sonia's turn.

As we touched down in Denver, the full impact of all that had transpired over the past two years—from the deaths of my father and brother to the separation to walking the Camino twice to this final unexpected and unwanted divorce—hit me like a tsunami. I found myself crying inconsolably before we even got the rental car.

In the car, on the way to the hotel, I went from sobbing uncontrollably to moaning in excruciating emotional pain to collapsing into sobs once again. I had never before felt like this, and, believe me, I had had some epic scenes in my life, given my Romanian blood. But this time took the cake.

As soon as we checked into the hotel, Sonia forced me to lie down on the bed and pulled the curtains. She then put a cold rag on my head and headed for the door. She was so sensitive that my breakdown was about to give her one, as well.

She needed to get away from me for a minute, as it was all too much for her to handle, and I agreed. Before she left, she asked me if she should take me to a hospital.

Normally, I would say no. This time, however, I didn't know the answer, and that scared me. I couldn't get it together the way I had been able to in past times of extreme stress.

"I can't go. I have to give a talk tonight," I replied. "But maybe I should, as I don't think I can give a talk tonight. I don't know. Pray for the answer."

"Well, we have a few hours to decide," Sonia said as she prepared to leave me in the darkened room. "It's only two now and you don't talk until seven tonight. So let's see if prayers work."

A few hours passed and I began to calm down. I had to show up and do a good job. I had to get it together. But how?

Just then Sonia came back to the hotel room and gingerly checked on me. She was both scared and overwhelmed. My falling apart was too much for her. She'd had enough loss. I couldn't be next. I knew it.

"Mom, are you feeling better?" she asked in the sweetest, most compassionate way that only my beautiful daughter could summon.

I just groaned. Everything in me wanted to say, *Yes, I'm fine. I'm sorry I fell apart today. No big deal. I'm as good as new. Forget about me flipping out. Please.*

"I hope so," I answered honestly.

Just then Sonia's cell phone rang. It was my Sabrina. Apparently, while I was resting, Sonia had given Sabrina an SOS phone call.

Handing me the phone, Sonia said, "Bean wants to talk to you."

"Hi, Bean," I said, my head now pounding with a splitting headache.

"Mom, listen to me. I heard from Sonia that you are losing it. I understand. You have just been dealt a lot and never expected this. But here's the deal. When I heard you were in trouble, I started praying to Mother Mary as I was driving along Lake Shore Drive, asking for her help. So here is what I got.

"I was told to give you a choice. We can take you to a hospital right now and you can have a nervous breakdown there. Or you can move to Paris. What's your choice? You have two minutes to decide."

I was shocked speechless by this proposition.

"You have nothing to lose, Mom," Sabrina continued. "You've just lost it all. I think you should listen to this guidance and move to Paris. I'll go with you. I need a new start, too. What do you say?"

I was quiet, breathing, taking in this crazy, wild, out-of-left-field suggestion. It was like getting a bucket of ice water thrown in my face.

A minute earlier, I could barely see the end of the bed I was lying in.

And suddenly, I could see Paris.

As if waking up from a nightmare, I thought, *If I am going to be traumatized, I might as well be traumatized in Paris, right?*

So, without a bit of hesitation, I said, "Okay, Sabrina. I hear you. Let's move to Paris. And soon. At least we can give it a try."

It was something to look forward to. It was divine guidance. The next step. And that's what I desperately needed right now.

I got up and washed my face. I could go on stage tonight and talk to people now. I could tell them what had happened. The Camino was healing, but the healing journey was not over yet. I could tell them that I got a divorce after all and did not get the happily-ever-after ending I thought was coming. I could tell them the truth, which I needed to do, and could only ever do.

But I could also tell them I was moving to Paris. And did.

A French Connection?

Once Sabrina and I decided to move to Paris, it was all systems go. Paris beckoned like a beautiful oasis in the desert of my now collapsed life. I had lived there before, 35 years earlier, when I attended the University of Paris on a study-abroad program in college, and made wonderful, lifelong friends during that time.

But even earlier than that, France had been a powerful spiritual home for me. The year before my study-abroad program, when I was working as a flight attendant, I was called to move to Aix-en-Provence in the south of France.

I couldn't explain the need to do this other than to say my spirit called me and I needed to follow. I felt a deep soul connection to the divine feminine in France, and for whatever reason my soul felt comforted when I was there, even if the rest of me felt seriously out of place and quite alone.

I was 21 years old. I quit my job and moved to Aix with only $500 in my pocket and an address of a place to stay, given to me by a fellow flight attendant whom I had casually met a few weeks earlier.

Four months after I arrived, I became very sick and ended up with a severe appendicitis attack and a double kidney infection the day before Christmas. So much for this big adventure.

I was whisked off to the hospital by my host family, who had found me on the floor in my tiny third-floor room, feverishly hallucinating, when they came upstairs to invite me for a holiday drink.

I spent 19 days in recovery after having my ruptured appendix removed. While in the local hospital, I shared a room with a 100-year-old woman called Mémé (pronounced "maymay" and meaning "grand-mother"), who was suffering from dementia and had broken her leg on Christmas day.

She was completely unconscious of me but talked nonstop to her angels, her family, her long-lost husband, her old enemies, ghosts, phantoms, and anyone else who danced through her mind while she lay there, immobile, in her cast. Listening to Mémé talk for all those days, I learned to speak French better than ever, albeit with a weird provincial accent.

My progress allowed me to eventually, through a series of wild events, test in and get a full-tuition scholarship to the Sorbonne in Paris the following year. It was all so weird and serendipitous that I knew I was meant to be in France. The doors just kept opening and pulling me in.

From the time I finished school all those years ago, I had returned to France, and especially Paris, almost every year.

My love of France did not end with me. When my daughters were little and started school, they attended the Lycée Français, or French School, in Chicago.

Moving to France therefore seemed the most logical thing to do after Armageddon. Sabrina was as comfortable in France as I was and needed just as big a change after ending a lengthy but unfulfilling relationship with her boyfriend in Los Angeles. Paris offered distance from our problems and a safe haven when all seemed so fragile and unclear.

The first order of the day was to find a place to stay, or at least a place to land and begin to sort out a new life once we were there.

Sabrina took over the job and dove into Airbnb. She scoured apartment after apartment, while reading about where the "cool" parts of Paris were these days.

After her careful research, we decided we would live in the 18th *arrondissement*, Montmartre, at the top of Paris near the Sacré-Cœur. The neighborhood overlooked the entire city and was apparently where the "cool" people hung out.

I was open to it, although when I lived in Paris all those years ago, it was a sketchy area full of sex shops and venues, which we usually avoided. Sabrina convinced me it was now the neighborhood where the bohemian chic congregated, so we figured we would feel right at home.

Bohemian chic or not, however, I wanted to be comfortable in our new place, especially given how raw my emotions were. While everything in me grabbed on to this move like a lifeline keeping me from drowning in my own pain, I still wanted—no, *needed*—to be comfortable.

Sabrina was on it, and within the week she found what was described on the Airbnb site as "a beautiful, luxurious two-bedroom apartment steps away from the Sacré-Cœur in the newly hip 18th" and at a price that couldn't be beat.

When she showed me the photo and read the description aloud, I was sold. "Let's book it for three months," I said. "We can start there and figure out the rest once we get there."

And with that it was settled.

Departures and Arrivals

The days leading up to our departure melted together into a gray fog. Focusing on so many practicalities as we readied ourselves to go, especially at the fire-drill pace at which we were moving, left no time, to think or worry about anything, past or future.

Packing for our move was challenging. Between the two of us, we had enough stuff to open a small clothing boutique and bedding shop. Shaking our heads at the mountain of "necessities" we had deemed essential to bring with us, we wondered what we would have packed if we were not being "sensible."

Knowing that in time we would eventually need to get long-stay visas, I began to research what that would require. The list was long and included having a lease on an apartment, for which an Airbnb did not qualify.

The countdown to leave was on. We were packed. The car was ordered. The Airbnb was in place. Our mountain of stuff was at the door. We were excited and ready to go.

Then the unthinkable happened. On January 7, two days before we were to leave, around 11:30 in the morning Paris time, two brothers, Saïd and Chérif Kouachi, forced their way into the Paris offices of a French satirical weekly newspaper, *Charlie Hebdo*, armed with assault rifles. They killed 12 people and injured many others.

Friends, family, and everyone who knew we were going begged us not to go.

And I would be lying if I didn't wonder if they were right. After all, things like this simply didn't happen in Paris. This was crazy. The entire city and beyond was in lockdown as the police hunted for the perpetrators. The siege of terror continued over the next two days as another terrorist killed a police officer and then showed up in a grocery store in the Jewish quarter and killed four more people.

Resolved to carry on with our plans, I reassured everyone that we would be fine. Our decision to go had never been a logical one. It was a soul calling, and because of that I fully trusted that we would be safe.

On the evening of January 9, we boarded United flight 985 from Chicago to Paris and set off for our new life.

When we arrived, the skies were overcast and very gray, with a light drizzle on the ground. We landed with a thud and stared at each other, wide-eyed, sharing an unspoken thought: *Oh my God, we're here.* Exchanging nervous smiles, we gathered our things and exited the plane, feeling both excited and anxious as we marched into this new adventure. Together we felt invincible.

At least until we hit baggage claim and had to manage our wagon train of luggage. When we were packing, I kept saying, "Thank God for Costco and these cheap, van-size suitcases."

It was another matter altogether now that we had to get these "vans" loaded onto the mini carts provided and out the door. Between the two of us, we had six large and three small suitcases, and the carts could hold only two each, given their size. Since the suitcases rolled, we each took a cart, stacked two large suitcases on it and balanced the little ones on top of those, and rolled another alongside.

It was a ridiculous arrangement that allowed us to move only inches at a time before one of the little suitcases would fall off the cart or the wheels of the suitcase alongside would jam, stopping our ramshackle wagon train dead in its tracks, and we would need to regroup all over again.

The fatigue, tension, and just plain aggravation of getting out the damn door set us off into one agitated argument after another.

"Mom, wait!" Sabrina screamed as I carefully rolled on ahead of her. Turning around I saw that two little suitcases had fallen off her loaded cart, and she was trying to collect them without losing her cool.

Turning to push my cart, it was my turn to lose it. The wheel of the rolling suitcase jammed and then collapsed.

"Shit! You've got to be kidding me," I groaned. "No wonder these suitcases were so cheap. They are just junk."

I was now forced to drag it alongside like a dead body, and my patience flew out the window. Both of us were exasperated by this fiasco. We looked at one another and burst out laughing.

"Why the hell did we bring so much stuff?" I asked.

Scanning the crowd in the terminal pick-up area, I searched for our driver, who I was informed would be waiting for us, holding a sign with my last name on it. No luck.

Obliged to drag our stuff farther away from the exit to avoid blocking traffic, I continued to look for our driver as we shuffled along.

"Enough," Sabrina snapped, tired of this monumental effort. "Let them walk around us. I'm not moving another inch." She'd had it. We parked the stuff with her, and I set off to look for our guy.

Just as I was about to give up, I saw him. There, across the hall, stood a bright, toothy, hugely smiling man of about 35, holding up a sign with my name on it. Once we made eye contact, he immediately set out in my direction.

"Madame Choquette?" he yelled out across the hall, waving the sign.

"*Oui,*" I answered, greatly relieved to see him. "*C'est moi.*"

Then he launched into English, which I really appreciated at the moment, as my brain felt like scrambled eggs and my ability to speak or think in French had flown straight out the door.

"Welcome to Paris," he said warmly and with genuine enthusiasm. "My name is Julien. I am your driver. Can I help you with your luggage?"

"Boy, can you ever," I answered, pointing to Sabrina a few feet away, buried under the mountain of stuff she was guarding.

"Wow," he said upon seeing what we had brought with us. "You Americans really travel with a lot on your vacation."

I laughed, then explained, "We are not just here for a short vacation, Julien. We are moving here."

"Wow," he said, not missing a beat, "You Americans move to a new country with very little stuff."

His sense of humor was just what we needed to ease the tension we were feeling. *"On y va,"* he said, relieving Sabrina of one of the carts, which meant, "Let's go," and marched ahead like a camp counselor, waving his hand in the air and leading us out the door to a huge van parked nearby.

I have been to Paris enough times in the past to know that having cheerful, helpful, delightful Julien show up was clearly the work of angels behind the scenes. Normally we would have encountered a surly and silent man who would do little to help. Julien, by contrast, was a huge calming force.

"Julien what an angel you are! Thank you for being so easygoing and helpful."

"No problem," he said. "Eets my plezzur!"

Sabrina and I exchanged glances and shared a silent prayer of thanks, then high-fived each other. We were on a great but uncertain adventure, and it was a relief to have support show up so quickly to assist us.

As we drove into town, Julien chatted away freely. He told us he was from Israel originally but had grown up mostly in Paris and loved his city, even though right now was a difficult moment to be there because of the recent attacks.

As we got closer, he said that where we were going to stay was, as he put it, "a very interesting" *quartier,* or neighborhood. "On one side of the street, you have the young bohemians who are very cool and hip," he explained, "and just across the street you have crack dens."

Sabrina and I looked at each other wide-eyed as he said this. Continuing nonchalantly, he said, "It will be very interesting to see what side of the street you will be on." Then he chuckled.

"The 18th is a mixture of African and Arab immigrants mostly," he said, "a lot of very poor people, and a lot of drugs and crime. But, as I said, if you are on the right side of the street, it is charming and cool, and, of course, very beautiful, with the Sacré-Cœur church at the top of Paris very nearby."

Listening to this, Sabrina and I became nervous. "What if we're on the wrong side of the street," I wondered out loud. Julien laughed and said, "Well then, you run very fast across the street."

We all laughed at that. As we approached the apartment, we saw droves of people streaming down the sidewalks, all appearing to be going in the same direction.

Before I could ask what was happening, Julien volunteered that today there was to be a *manifestation*—a demonstration—at the Place de la République in honor of national unity and denouncing the recent terrorist attacks. He said almost everyone in Paris was expected to be there, millions in fact, and world leaders were expected to show up as well. He himself was going as soon as he dropped us off. It was his duty as a French national to be there.

As we got closer we got to the apartment, I could see what he meant by the neighborhood being shaky. There were a lot of young and old men standing around in groups, smoking cigarettes, some yelling at each another in Arabic from the doorways in which they stood, looking angry and agitated. It was definitely *not* the beautiful scene that typically pops into your head when dreaming of Paris. The *quartier* was crammed with makeshift shops and ethnic fast food restaurants, their greasy smells hovering in the air. Garbage was strewn about the streets, and there were random ugly splotches of red and black graffiti defacing the buildings, assaulting our senses, and blasting us out of our fantasy about living in "beautiful Paris."

"Are you sure we are in the right area?" I asked.

"Yep," said Julien as he pulled up to a building and parked the car.

"Welcome. You are home!" he announced brightly, pointing to a building on the left. "And guess what?" he added. "Lucky you! You are on the right side of the street. Just don't go over there," he said, pointing to the other side, "and you'll be fine."

Part Two

THE OLD LADY

Home Sweet New Home

I had been to Paris many times over the years and had lived here with a family for a year when I went to the Sorbonne, but this was a neighborhood I had never spent much time in, and now I could see why. It looked intense, ungrounded, and a little scary.

It was a far cry from the vast open spaces, green parks, and gorgeous buildings that one typically thinks of as Paris. But then again, nothing was typical about our arriving here, especially now. I was shattered, Paris was shattered, and, by the look of things, this neighborhood was also shattered. We seemed to go together.

As Julien started to unload the bags, I opened the front door to the solid gray stone building that was our new home, using the code that the apartment host had given us, and stepped into the ground-floor foyer, or *rez de chaussée* as it is known in France. Inside was an oasis of calm.

I searched for a light, as it was pitch-dark, and found a switch to the right of the front door. Our eyes were greeted by a wide hall with cracking gold-speckled mirrors lining both sides leading up to a second set of doors with a tiny little elevator on the other side. Again, using a code the host had provided, I unlocked the second set of doors and propped them open using the small suitcases.

By the time I turned around, Julien had shoved the last bag into the foyer. "Good luck, ladies. Be safe," he said with a cheerful wave. And off he went.

Sabrina and I looked at one another, the reality of the moment fully hitting us. "Well, here we are," I said, remaining optimistic. "Home sweet home." She laughed and retorted, "Let's hope so."

Forging ahead in spite of our reservations about the neighborhood, our next task was to get the bags upstairs to our second-floor apartment, where the host was supposed to meet us with the apartment key.

Eyeing what had to be the tiniest elevator I had ever seen in my life, I quickly discerned that there was no way we could fit more than one bag into the elevator at a time, so we devised a system on the spot.

"I'll run upstairs and wait while you load the bags and send them up," I said to Sabrina. "When the last bag is on the elevator, just walk up and meet me."

The winding staircase leading upstairs was wide and well worn and shone from years and years of use, the wood on the steps gleaming from polish. The building was quite old but had a regal charm and seemed to command respect.

Unlike the neighborhood outside the front door, where there was a multicultural free-for-all going on, the inside of this solid stone building oozed old-world and *quiet* French dignity and charm. It was obviously deeply loved and cared for by whoever locked all those doors and polished all those stairs.

"Okay, Mom, I'll start loading," Sabrina said as I turned and began to head up. At the top I met the elevator and began unloading the bags, one elevator full at a time.

There were two apartments on each floor, with a small landing between them. I was careful not to be too loud as it was Sunday, typically a day when everyone is home, and I didn't want to make a bad impression on the neighbors.

Just when the last bag was unloaded and Sabrina arrived upstairs, our apartment host showed up with the key. Well, it wasn't exactly our host, as he was a French film producer who lived in Brooklyn. This woman, Angélique, was his agent in Paris.

She was very warm and welcoming, but I couldn't help notice how aghast she looked when she saw the mountain of luggage we had stacked up in front of the door.

She casually remarked, as she unlocked the door, "You are staying here for only three months, *no?*"

"Yes, that's right," we said. "Three months."

Les Pigeons

Undeterred by the neighborhood, Sabrina and I were eager to enter our new "luxury" digs and could hardly wait until Angélique opened the door to the apartment. After all, the two photos on the Airbnb site had made it seem very beautiful.

Once the door was opened and we walked into the entryway, however, we came face to face with the un-Photoshopped reality. A dingy glass wall ran from floor to ceiling straight ahead. On the other side was an atrium that led from the ground up to the top floor, six stories above us. Inside this atrium cooed and fluttered what seemed like a thousand stinky pigeons, which were staring in and looking straight at us.

We were almost thrown backward by the smell. Angélique instantly apologized, saying, "I know. It's a leetel problem. But you get used to it."

Dumbfounded, as this was the last thing we expected and was certainly *not* featured in the Airbnb photos or description, we stood motionless, staring at the pigeons staring at us, and then finally at each other, at a total loss as to how to react.

This lasted for a full 20 seconds before Angélique shook us out of our shock by asking if we wanted to see the rest of the apartment.

"Sure," we said in a mild daze, and followed her to the main room. There, under 12-foot ceilings and with typically French chalk-white wall paint, was a large double parlor. In one half was a very large, low-lying couch draped in a messy gray linen cover, facing a huge TV mounted on the wall over a marble fireplace mantel. Behind the couch, in the other half, was a large, beautiful, solid stone dining-room table that seated 12 people, along with a few cheap floor lamps and an ancient and rickety cabinet filled with a few mismatched dishes.

On the back wall was a large oil painting of a bucolic country scene, and a few *papier-mâché* statues of Asian soldiers stood on a table in the corner. At the far end of the room were three large floor-to-ceiling windows that flooded the apartment with light. Covered with sheer white linen drapes, they overlooked the sketchy neighborhood, allowing us to see both sides of the street. They were the saving grace of the apartment and drew us in like flies to honey.

I marveled at how some clever photographer had made these two rooms look so much grander, larger, and more luxurious than they actually were. The photographer's creativity obviously worked, as here we were.

Still speechless, Sabrina and I followed Angélique as she led us past the atrium once again and toward the back of the apartment.

"Here is the bathroom," she said, pointing to the left at a tiny room next to the atrium and across from the kitchen. In it was a small shower, a sink, and a tiny clothes washer on the floor underneath the countertop. Tucked on the other side of the atrium was an even smaller room with a toilet. "And here is the kitchen," she continued, turning and pointing to her right at an alcove the size of an airplane galley, with a tabletop stove across from a double oven, a half-size refrigerator, and a tiny window in the corner. It had everything you needed, only miniature.

Continuing the tour, we stepped two more feet to the back of the apartment and saw the two bedrooms the listing had advertised.

In fact, it was one bedroom with a makeshift wall down the middle, technically creating two rooms but leaving each so small it could barely accommodate a bed—a single on one side, a double on the other—let alone our suitcases. Each little room had a floor-to-ceiling window next to the bed. It was tight quarters to say the least.

"These are the two bedrooms?" I asked Angélique incredulously.

"Yes," she said, looking at me as if wondering what I could possibly mean.

"They are awfully small," I said as we peered in—it was not possible for all three of us to enter at the same time. My mind momentarily drifted to the huge master bedroom and bathroom with Jacuzzi tub I had just left behind in Chicago, and I wondered for a split second what on earth I had been thinking to exchange that for this.

"They are normal size for Paris," she insisted. And I knew she meant it.

"Okay," I said, taking a deep breath. "Well then, that's that."

"Oh, I do have one more question," I said, remembering, as Angélique headed for the door. "Where are the closets?"

"Closets?" she asked as if I were out of my mind. "We have no closets here."

"Where do we put our clothes, then?" I asked, thinking of the mountain of stuff still waiting in the hall outside the door.

"Oh, here," she said, leading us back to the stinky atrium by the front door and pointing to a wall of IKEA cubicles stacked on top of one another from floor to ceiling. "You have a lot of storage space." She beamed, happy to show us what she was sure was the best feature in our glamorous new pad. "You can put all of your things here."

Sabrina and I looked at the wall in disbelief. What had we gotten ourselves into? And paid for in full for the next three months?

I didn't know whether to laugh or cry.

"One last thing," she said just before leaving. "You turn this on for heat." She pointed to a small electric heater plugged into the wall in the living room. "But you must turn it off when you leave and at night. Otherwise you must pay the extra amount for the heating bill, and it is very expensive."

Just then I realized we still had our winter coats on and could almost see our breath in the apartment it was so cold.

"Okay, got it," I answered. "No problem."

She then handed us the keys and told us to feel free to call her if we needed anything, although she was a schoolteacher and could only answer after school and on weekends.

Once she was gone, we dragged our suitcases inside the apartment and piled them against the wall, then plopped ourselves down on the couch, still trying to fully absorb it all. After a few minutes of silence, we both shrugged our shoulders, looked at each other, and said, nearly at the same time, "Well, here we are. We will just have to make it work."

Resolved not to allow our disappointment in the place to get us down, I added, "Hey, it's Paris. How bad can it be?"

Then suddenly Sabrina started to laugh really hard, "You know what, Mom? This apartment looks and smells like an old lady."

"Oh my God, Sabrina. You are so right!" I said, laughing along with her. "That's what we are going to call this place: the Old Lady."

Then we unzipped our coats, walked over to the large windows, and threw them open to let in some sorely needed fresh air.

Solidarity

By the time Angélique left, it was nearly two in the afternoon, and we suddenly realized we were starving. "Come on," I said to Sabrina, fighting fatigue from the flight. "Let's find a place for lunch and then maybe get a few things for the apartment."

Since we were only on the second floor, we decided to walk down the winding staircase instead of cramming into the tiny elevator. We started down and I nearly slipped on the slick, worn stairs.

Winding our way back down, we saw that there were two apartments on each floor and a small courtyard at the bottom, which led to a place for garbage. On the left, in the *rez de chaussée,* was the apartment belonging to the *gardien,* the person in charge of watching the building. In Paris, almost every building has one. The *gardien's* job is to take care of the building, keep it clean, receive packages, and watch over everything that happens, to make sure all is well. I have been in buildings where the *gardien* was like a pit bull, guarding the building with his or her life, scaring me to death every time I passed by, and in buildings where the *gardien* was pleasant and easygoing, a pleasure to chat with. They were always very formal in any case, and it was best to be on good terms with them if you were going to get past them, let alone live in the building. We would definitely stop by later and introduce ourselves, but for the moment we were too tired and hungry to do that.

Once outside, we were met with people pouring past us in droves. Entire families of all ethnicities, kids in strollers, large groups of friends, old people and young, all streaming toward the Place de la République, the large square located in the 10th arrondisement, about a mile from where we were, and the epicenter of the *manifestation* against the terrorist acts. Julien had said the entire city would be there, and from what we could see, it was true. Everyone was walking in that direction.

Following our stomachs instead of the crowd, we navigated against the flow of traffic and headed around the corner. Soon we found ourselves heading up a steep flight of stairs and toward the top of Montmartre, the Sacré-Cœur, the neighborhood on the hill at the top of the city. Made up of small, winding streets filled with charming cafés, boutiques, and restaurants, mostly catering to tourists these days, it was so fascinating and colorful we nearly forgot about our jet lag and our "luxurious" apartment.

In the early 19th century, Montmartre was filled with small artists' studios, nightclubs, and cabarets. In the late 19th and early 20th centuries, during what was known as the Belle Époque, it was home to famous artists such as Salvador Dali, Modigliani, Monet, Toulouse-Lautrec, Mondrian, Pissarro, Picasso, and Van Gogh. It later went into decline, and during the year I had been a student here, it was more a place to avoid than an attraction. Over the past few years, however, Montmartre enjoyed a huge renaissance as young artists and hip entrepreneurs opened pop-up shops, art galleries, trendy restaurants, and hip cafés there. These abutted the more traditional ones, with their Belle Époque décor and classic menus, creating a delightful cool-meets-classic Paris feel.

As we wandered around, we immediately revived. Everywhere we looked was beautiful, fascinating, mysterious, and enticing. I felt like Alice having just stepped through the looking glass into Wonderland as we passed café after café, not quite sure which one to enter as they all looked so inviting. Even on this brisk, cold January day, chairs and tables were outside, beckoning us to sit and enjoy a break. I imagined that normally the chairs would be filled with people relaxing and enjoying a leisurely Sunday lunch, but this was not an ordinary day.

Within minutes we found ourselves looking into a minuscule café with only four tables inside and the smell of roasting garlic and hot bread wafting from the kitchen.

"Let's eat here," Sabrina said. "I'm too hungry and too tired to look any further." I agreed. I, too, was running out of gas and jet lag was catching up. More than food, what I really needed was a big cup of café au lait if I was to keep going.

Luckily for us, the café was nearly empty. Looking at the menu, we were thrilled to see asparagus and garlic soup with crème fraîche, which was no doubt the delicious smell that pulled us in, and a *salade du moment* (of the day), which today was green leafy lettuce, baby shrimp, fresh avocado, and small pieces of grape-fruit. We were sold.

We quickly ordered soups and salads, along with two large bowls of café au lait, which earned us a startled scowl, as that was clearly something you drank only in the morning here. We didn't care. The food and café au lait were so good, it felt as though we were eating in a gourmet five-star restaurant instead of a tiny café hidden away on a side street near the *butte.*

"Oh my God, Sabrina, this soup is soothing my soul," I said, nearly inhaling the entire bowl at once.

"I know," she said. "It's fantastic. I want to order a second bowl."

"Me too."

"Thank you, angels," we both said aloud, definitely feeling the presence of loving, unseen forces guiding our way as we ventured into this next episode of our lives.

This Paris was not the innocent Paris we had known in the past. The Paris before the attacks felt safe, an oasis of beauty and art, creativity, possibility, and inspiration. That is what brought us here. We felt it would soothe our raw, aching souls. After the terrorist attacks, however, Paris felt so deeply wounded, so blind-sided, so ambushed with hatred, it was devastating. And confus-ing. Such things didn't happen here. Until now, anyway.

Drinking our second cups of café au lait, I looked at Sabrina and said, "We need to go to the Place de la République and join the rest of the city. This is our home now, too, and we need to lend our voices to the cry for peace and unity."

"You're right," she said. "Let's go."

We paid our bill and left, and started to follow along with the others streaming toward the Place de la République, the symbolic heart and soul of France. As we walked, the impact of all that had just transpired, both here in Paris and in my life, suddenly hit me and slammed me back into my body.

"I don't know why, but I don't think it's an accident that we arrived today of all days. It certainly helps me to see past my own pain. At least right now."

Tears started streaming down my face, catching me by surprise. Walking alongside the masses of shocked, scared, wounded, angry people hurt my heart. We may have had different reasons for joining the *manifestation,* but in the end, we felt the same, refusing to relinquish our light to the darkness.

We arrived at the Place de la République 45 minutes later. In the middle of the grand, open plaza stands a huge bronze statue of an allegorical figure, Marianne, embodying the French Republic and its motto, "Liberty, Equality, Fraternity." She symbolizes the pride of the French people and the values they hold so dear to their hearts.

Thousands of people were assembled, of every age, every color, and every class, all chanting, *"Tous ensemble, Chrétiens, Juifs, Musulmans,"* which meant, "All together, Christians, Jews, and Muslims."

The base of the statue was covered with candles and lots of young people had climbed onto it and were chanting from the top. People surrounding the statue started linking arms and singing the national anthem at the top of their lungs as the night sky descended upon us. Some raised their fists as they chanted, *"Nous sommes tous ensemble,"* meaning, "We are all together." Not one person remained silent. Even the little kids in the crowd cried out with the rest.

A klezmer band played on one end of the plaza, and a reggae band played at the other end. Thousands of people were holding lit candles as they chanted and sang, as it was now already beginning to get dark, even though it was only 4:30 P.M.

The place lit up like a festival, but the mood was far from festive. It was defiant and fearless. "We won't be afraid." "We won't be intimidated." "We won't darken our light." "We live for peace and unity." All of this was chanted, but the chant we heard more than any other was, *"Je suis Charlie Hebdo."* As we walked we noticed signs bearing the same words plastered on store windows, lamp posts, benches, everywhere. It seemed it had become the national motto for freedom. While the magazine was attacked by Islamist extremists for insulting Islam, the people of France chanted this cry to say they would not tolerate anything less than absolute freedom of the press and freedom of speech, ideals that they hold dear and close to their hearts. To be here meant we, too, were *Charlie Hebdo.*

Bienvenue, Mesdames

Once we arrived back at the apartment, it was freezing. The tiny heater did little to warm up the space.

Ha! Not to worry. Sticklers for comfort that we were, we had both brought down comforters with us. Friends had told us we were crazy for having packed them; now we felt vindicated.

Sabrina walked into her little room on the far side of the make-shift wall. It was tight quarters, but she said it would be fine. We laughingly tried to both fit around the bed as we struggled to make it up. We then did the same for my bed on the other side.

We next opened our other suitcases and fished out our paja-mas. Sabrina had a few protein bars in her bag, which we munched on as we sat on the large couch facing the blank TV, getting used to the place. We resolved that it was a great little apartment despite having pigeons for roommates, and it just needed a little TLC and a few strong-scented candles to make it feel like home sweet home.

We lasted another hour, but by 8 P.M. we were ready for bed. We said good night, and I crawled into bed and passed out. A few hours later, Sabrina suddenly woke me up out of a dead sleep.

"Mom, move over. I have to sleep in here," she said, startling me.

"Okay, why?" I asked, not sure if I was dreaming.

"It's freezing on my side of the wall, and I'm above a bar with a lot of drunk people outside. It's so loud I can't sleep."

I had been in such a deep sleep, I just rolled over and mum-bled, "Sure, get in. And bring your comforter. I'm freezing, too."

Two minutes later we were both unconscious, wrapped around each other in an exhausted attempt to stay warm.

The next morning, we were up at dawn. Sabrina said she was going to take a shower while I started to unpack our belongings. I stared at the wall of cubicles in front of me, trying to figure out how on earth we were going to manage to put all our stuff into such small spaces.

A few minutes later, I heard a scream.

"What's wrong?" I asked, running into the bathroom, only to find Sabrina sitting on the shower floor. "Why are you sitting down there? Did you let the water run long enough to warm up?"

"Yes, I did," she said, shampoo dripping from her hair into her eyes. "It was hot a minute ago. It just stopped and now it's like ice water. And I'm on the floor because the showerhead is too low to stand under it." I could see what she meant.

Laughing at her soap-filled head leaning away from the ice bucket pouring down on her from a showerhead clearly set up for someone four feet tall, I said, "Suck it up, Bean. Pretend you're at camp and rinse off as fast as you can."

"Shit!" she screamed, eyes squeezed tightly shut. "This sucks. What happened to the hot water?"

Looking overhead, I saw the smallest water heater I've ever seen, to go along with every other Lilliputian element in the apartment.

"The Old Lady ran out," I said.

Rinsing off with lightning speed, she jumped out of the shower, shivering to the bone. Grabbing a towel, she didn't know whether to laugh or be angry. "That is *not* how I wanted to start my day."

I just shook my head. "Sabrina, apparently we are not in Kansas anymore."

Twenty minutes later, we were dressed and eager to explore the area. The first thing on the agenda was to find a café and get some breakfast. We were starving.

Using her handy guide to Paris on her iPhone, Sabrina led us to a café around the corner and a few blocks toward the Sacré-Cœur. In a matter of only five minutes, our walk went from poor-immigrant Paris to quaint and charming Belle Époque Paris.

As we approached our intended café on rue Lepic, we noticed several small tables in front filled with men in long, dark overcoats and scarves elegantly wrapped around their necks, smoking cigarettes, sipping espressos. Some were reading newspapers, others were chatting with one another, while still others were just watching the world go by. All appeared oblivious to the cold.

Far too cold to join them, we went inside and sat on a red leather banquette along the window. The walls were covered in gilded mirrors with hand-painted panels and ornate sconces in between them. There were small tables throughout and a long zinc bar at one end, behind which stood a man taking coffee orders and talking with a few more men standing around it. It was right out of a movie.

We waited for a very long time before the only waiter on the premises came over to serve us. Slamming the menus down in front of us, he turned and left before we could even say "Good morning."

If that had happened in the U.S., we would have been very insulted, but this was France. It was normal.

Five minutes later he returned. *"Je vous écoute"* ("I'm listening"), he barked, not looking at us, his body only half facing us, as if ready to walk away midsentence.

We rushed with our order. "Two omelets, two café au laits, and a croissant." By the time we got to the croissant, he was already two steps away.

Why is he so rushed? We're the only ones inside! we eyeballed to each other, glancing around, remembering we were in Paris. More or less all the waiters acted like this. I never understood why, but I wasn't going to let him annoy me. It was much too exciting to be here, and much too early in the morning to let his gruff affect get me down.

Five minutes later he slammed down my croissant and the most delicious omelets in the world, perfectly seasoned with a bit of tarragon and a dash of Emmental cheese and as fluffy as pancakes.

"Et voilà!" he proclaimed, and off he went once again.

The croissant was still warm and so flaky and buttery it melted in my mouth. *Uh-oh,* I immediately thought, licking my fingers. *This is too good. I had better watch it or I am going to get fat on these things.* It was so scrumptious, I nearly inhaled it.

Then came two large bowls of café au lait, hot espresso with steamed milk. When it comes to coffee in Paris, it's hit or miss. Sometimes it is really delicious, and sometimes it's just "bleh."

We were in luck. Today it was delicious. And hot enough, which is my pet peeve. I've ordered café au laits all over France over the years, and most of the time they are barely lukewarm and I have to either drink them like that, to my disappointment, or summon my courage to send them back and ask for them to be warmed up. It's always intimidating to send something back, and getting what I want depends on how much I want to push for it, which is, more often than not, not a lot.

"What a great start to the day, Sabrina. Good omelet. Good café au lait. A fabulous, buttery croissant. I'm happy. Let's check out the neighborhood and get some groceries after this," I said, sipping on my second bowl of coffee, fortified for the day ahead.

Our next challenge was to pay the bill. We sat and sat, but still could not get the waiter's attention to get our bill. It seemed as though he did everything in the world to avoid making eye contact with us and, after dropping off the second round of café au laits, had forgotten we were even there.

We tried in vain to get his attention and even waved our hands in the air, all to no avail. He talked with the barista, walked to and fro, from the inside to the outside, scanned the restaurant, and placed napkins and silverware on the surrounding tables. Finally, after a full 15 minutes of this, I gave up and walked up to the bar and asked for our check, not realizing that this game of "get the check" would be one we would play on an almost daily basis from now on.

Two minutes later, the waiter came up to the table, dropped the check on a small plate in front of us, and once again started to walk away.

"S'il vous plaît, Monsieur," I cried out before he got too far. "We want to pay *now*," I said in French, and he stopped, turned around, and came back. Feeling really rushed before he ran away again, I grabbed some money and thrust it at him as fast as I could. He took the bill and reached into his vest pocket for the change, slapping it on the small plate before us, tearing the bill a little, and handing it back to us. *"Et, voilà,"* he pronounced just as he did with the omelets, then turned and walked away once again before we could say another word.

We walked out not knowing whether we loved the place or didn't. The food was great. The coffee was hot. The waiter was annoying. We decided we loved the place.

We just couldn't be sensitive Americans, I reasoned to myself, if we were to be happy here. We had to observe how the Parisians did things and follow suit. And we had to remember to take nothing personally. Given how vulnerable and overly sensitive we both were now, however, that was going to be a challenge.

Running on adrenaline and caffeine, we then set off to discover our new, "hip" neighborhood and get some necessities for the apartment.

Wandering back to our corner, at the top of des rues de Clignancourt and Christiani, just above boulevard Barbès-Rochechouart, was a colorful experience. We saw beautiful, tall African women in traditional colorful cotton dresses with gorgeous matching head wraps pushing strollers with babies, older kids running alongside, laden with bags, music blaring from small radios dangling on their strollers as they went about their morning errands.

On the way down rue de Clignancourt toward the boulevard was a huge department store called Tati, a cheaper version of Target and our first destination. Just outside the store, groups of Muslim men wearing floor-length brown robes sat on plastic boxes that served as chairs, prayer beads in hand, some staring in silence, others talking animatedly with one another while smoking cigarettes, and others selling cheap suitcases stacked up high on the sidewalk behind them.

Overhead and across from Tati was the métro, and underneath it was an intensely busy fresh market, jam-packed with people from all over the world. It was spellbinding to hear the vendors' calls among the crowd in both Arabic and French as North Africans, Parisians, and tourists pushed their way through the crowd. We wanted to check it out but were too intimidated to attempt this just yet. "Maybe in a few days," we reasoned, "when we feel more grounded."

In Tati, we stocked up on laundry and dish soap, cheap towels, napkins, sponges, paper towels, and more. The most important item we bought was a rolling grocery cart—known as a *chariot* in French—into which we put all our items, knowing it would come in handy every time we went shopping for food and other necessities.

It felt comforting to stock up on cleaning items. I've always needed to work from a solid foundation, and since I presently had no foundation *whatsoever*, cleaning the apartment would at least allow me to get grounded and feel more relaxed in the Old Lady.

Equipped with every sort of cleaning supply imaginable now, and rolling "Chariot" behind us, we wandered back up the street toward home, closely studying the scene every inch of the way. Most of the shops along Clignancourt were devoted to wholesale hair products, and it occurred to me that this must be the district, or at least one of the districts, where hairdressers came to buy their supplies. There were lots of specialized districts like this in Paris, where all the shops sold more or less the same type of products. Most of the hair products on display in these shops were, not surprisingly, for African hair. There were also a few hair salons, a nail shop, a few more suitcase shops sprinkled in, along with an exterminator's shop with a few dead rats and mice hanging in the window in case anyone needed proof that they knew what they were doing. In the middle of the stretch home was a larger grocery store, Carrefour City Market, one of the main grocery chains in the city, where we decided we would return later to pick up some basics for dinner.

Just past the grocery store, sitting on a flattened cardboard box surrounded by a few bags, was a family of four. There was a young father of about 30, a mother with a scarf on her head, a little boy who appeared to be about four or five, and an infant sitting in the father's lap. It was freezing outside and they barely had on any warm clothes.

My heart leapt into my throat. *Jesus. Is this their home?* I wondered.

Smiling, the father stuck out a tattered, filthy paper cup and asked for a donation. I dug deep into my pocket and gave him all the coins I had, appalled that this was where they lived.

He seemed very grateful and thanked me profusely. I felt terrible for them, and yet, walking away, I couldn't help but remark that they didn't seem all that miserable, in spite of their condition.

I had no idea who they were or why they were on the street. They could have been a gypsy family, or they could have been refugees. Maybe they were just a French family down on their luck. It was hard to tell just by looking at them. Who knows? They were laughing and playing and having a good time, however, and that is what struck me the most. Talk about making the most out of a bad situation. I could learn from them.

Continuing up to the top of our street, we came upon a beautiful flower shop, an oasis of elegance and grace snuggled between a combined cell phone/Chinese take-out place and a *boulangerie,* or bakery.

Seeing it, I was reminded of one of the reasons I love Paris so much. In Paris, beauty is a not an indulgence, it is a necessity, something as important as food and oxygen. Maybe more so. Parisians seem to understand that beauty feeds and heals the soul and that we need it to survive. And fresh flowers were part of that beauty. Parisians bought flowers like they bought bread. It was part of their diet, a staple in their lives. I wanted flowers to be a staple in mine now.

The shop was owned by a kind Arab man, who smiled brightly as we looked over the various offerings in his store. Gorgeous violet and white orchids, roses in every imaginable color, bursts of freesia, and sweet bouquets of exotic flowers filled the air with such a lovely fragrance that it was intoxicating. It was like a candy store made of flowers.

When it was finally our turn (the owner took his time with each customer, and they took their time, as well), we introduced ourselves and told him we had just moved in across the street. He was kind and friendly, and welcomed us warmly, saying his name was Fayyad. We then told him we were in need of two fragrant bouquets because our apartment smelled like pigeons, which made him laugh out loud. He then lovingly created two fabulous and fragrant bouquets made of white lilies, freesia, and eucalyptus for us, carefully wrapping them in ribbons and greenery, then sent us on our way, saying, *"Bienvenue, mesdames, et bon courage,"* meaning, "Welcome to the neighborhood, ladies, and good luck."

Happy to have all we needed to freshen up the Old Lady, we went back and spent the rest of the day making our new apartment feel more like home.

In spite of the pigeons, in spite of the lack of heat, in spite of the raucous bar beneath Sabrina's room and the cold water and the absence of closets and the teeny-tiny everything, we were content. We could do this. We lived in Paris now. We could hardly believe it.

Soul Medicine

Our top priority was getting set up for work. Both Sabrina and I worked with our clients over the phone, which allowed us to live abroad. Only now, we had to figure out how we could both manage to work at the same time, given the apartment had no doors save for the bedrooms, only one phone, and Internet only in the front end.

We devised a plan in which I would work on the phone in the back of the apartment, nestled in the corner of the kitchen, and Sabrina would work in the dining room at the other end of the apartment, near the front window, using Skype. That way we were far enough away from each other to work in privacy. After a trial run, we were relieved to discover that this arrangement worked perfectly and business could go on as usual.

The only glitch in our setup was that I did an Internet radio show every week at 6 P.M., which required that I get into the dining room where the equipment and Internet were and plug the phone and my radio equipment into the phone jack, while Sabrina had to clear out.

That meant that every Wednesday at 5:57 P.M. sharp we went into a mad dash, her rushing out and me rushing in, with only seconds to spare before I was live on the radio. Needless to say, there was a lot of confusion and clashing between us during this rapid shift change, as the pressure was on.

"Hurry, Sabrina! I have to start," I said, as she shut down her computer. Flinging her computer cord out of the wall socket, shoving mine in, and snapping the radio line in place of the telephone, with only seconds to spare, I was on.

Ten seconds later the show began.

On one occasion, my own call with a client went over and cut the time to get ready for the show so close I thought I would blow it. I ran into the dining room and exploded into a panicked whisper-scream to Sabrina to help me out fast, just as she was hanging up.

We frantically fumbled plugs and cords, both screaming at each other as we did. Just then music swelled and the show went live, stopping us both in midsentence.

"Hello, everyone," I greeted my listeners in as smooth a voice as I could muster. "Today's topic is, 'Take a breath.'" The minute I said that, Sabrina burst out laughing, which caused me to do the same. I put my hand over the microphone as she shook her head at me and mouthed, "You are so ridiculous!" Shooing her out of the room as I struggled to regain my composure, I asked my listeners to join me in taking a few deep breaths right away, telling them my day was rushed and I needed to do this myself, just so I could settle down and begin the show calmly.

Working with my clients every day was my daily refuge. When I unplugged from my own life and tuned in to helping others, I changed my inner channel and became instantly calm and clear. It was the one aspect of my life in which I had no confusion. When doing my intuitive work, it was as though I had an aerial view and could see clearly and forever, helping guide those on the ground to get to where they were going in the most graceful way possible. It was just that when it came to my own life, the channel switched back and it felt as though I were trying to follow my intuition under water. I was still following my inner guidance, only I couldn't see five feet ahead. Like a submarine submerged in choppy seas, I was forging ahead on pure vibration alone.

More than once I wondered how on earth we ended up in such a strange and challenging situation in this not-very-beautiful immigrant section of Paris. Granted, we were only minutes away from the winding streets of Montmartre, with its bohemian flair and endless appeal, at the top of the city, but we were more immersed in the reality of today's post–*Charlie Hebdo* terrorist attack African-Arab Paris than we were in the Toulouse-Lautrec romantic Paris of the past. On some days, the harsh reality was overwhelming.

Almost daily, as we wound our way back to the apartment after getting our groceries or a morning café au lait, we witnessed French policeman rounding up groups of immigrants and checking their papers, often with guns pointed. It was shocking and disturbing and hard to accept. In my mind, Paris was the city of beauty and serenity, not this.

Being immigrants ourselves at the moment, my heart ached for the people being checked. Everyone was scared. I could see it in their faces. The mostly young cops looked as scared as the people they rounded up, many of them appearing to be in their early 20s. It was obvious they didn't like doing this any more than the people they were checking did. It was painful for everyone and distressing to witness.

On top of all this, as much as I didn't want to acknowledge it, the devastation and misery I had just experienced from the divorce followed me to Paris. While grateful for the change of scenery, I felt as though I had just been in a terrible accident, an emotional hit-and-run, and was sent to Paris for soul rehabilitation.

I was so lost inside it was difficult to find my bearings. Being married for more than 30 years had forged a "married" identity in me. Not being married felt as though my arm had just been cut off. It was weird and disconcerting and created a deep ache in me that I just couldn't soothe. Some essential part of me was now missing, and I was left with phantom-limb symptoms that haunted me all the time.

It didn't matter that my Higher Self said this was all for the highest good of all concerned. It didn't matter that, on an intuitive level, I knew I had to walk a separate path from here on out. It didn't matter that, from a spiritual perspective, I knew this was part of my soul journey and I had lessons to learn from the experience. It didn't even matter that, on a deep intuitive level, I was grateful for this ending and was happy it finally occurred.

Right now all that mattered was that I hurt deeply and desperately wanted to feel better. I was faced with the need to start over, to walk away from the ashes, and to begin again. It seemed an insurmountable challenge. Thank God I wasn't alone in having to face it. At least for now.

In her own way, Sabrina was in the same boat as I was. She, too, had just exited a long-term relationship of six years. Like me, she'd ended the life she had created—hers in Los Angeles with her partner and beloved little dog, Sneaker—and left her home behind.

We were an emotional mess. One of us would become suddenly cranky and reactive or burst into tears or fall into a moody funk, then the other would freak out. Then we would argue and both go up in flames.

Our only antidote for all this pain and confusion was to go for long walks through Paris every night after work and enjoy a simple dinner together. It became our daily soul medicine. In fact, we walked so much it felt as though we were walking the equivalent of another Camino every night. Starting at the top of Paris, where our apartment was located, we set out for a new destination each night. We walked from Montmartre to the Opéra, to the Bastille, to the Panthéon, to the Jardin du Luxembourg, to the Seine, to the Marais, to the Place de la République, to Notre Dame, and back, taking a new route each time. The novelty of everything we saw provided a distraction from our battered emotions, while the movement helped to ease their fragments out of our bones.

Unlike in America, where streets are generally uniformly laid out and everything feels more or less modern and predictable, Paris is a series of small villages, each with its own flavor and color and unique personality, none of it predictable, most of it ancient, mysterious, and full of surprises. For centuries, this veritable buffet of sensory input prompted artists and poets to stroll the streets, seeking aesthetic inspiration—so much so that they acquired their own name: *flaneurs*.

Each nightly walk was like a treasure hunt. The streets wound every which way, seducing us with their mysteries. Oftentimes we happened upon something so strange and unexpected it stopped us in our tracks.

For example, one night we wandered into the second arrondissement, just past place des Victoire, and turned onto rue Aboutir. There we came across a taxidermy shop filled with huge stuffed wild animals straight off the savanna, displayed in the window of a very large store. There was an ostrich, a lion, a gorilla, several large birds, a rhinoceros, and even a stuffed giraffe inside. It was the equivalent of an exotic safari on display. In the window was also a sign that said all the animals in the shop had died in their natural habitat from natural causes before they were stuffed, which was somehow relieving, even though it still seemed disturbing to see those magnificent animals staring at us from behind a window in Paris. Still, we were fascinated and couldn't pull our eyes away for quite a while.

We ran across shops at the place Colette displaying old coins, war medals, antique jewelry, little metal army men, bizarre lighting fixtures of every shape imaginable, as well as pop-up clothing boutiques, specialty paper shops, pen shops, shoe shops, cheese shops, perfume shops, bakeries, pillow shops, lingerie shops, wine shops, tea shops, map shops, and on and on, all interspersed between quaint cafés, bistros, restaurants, and nightclubs.

I have always found shopping to be a spiritual experience, especially in foreign cities, so every night I window-shopped my way to heaven and back, feeding both my soul and my imagination with all the beautiful, quirky, and sometimes downright strange things I saw along the way. Our nocturnal walking meditations were like salve on my open wounds, and each nightly foray eased the pain in my heart ever so slightly.

Ça Va?

Mornings started with a 15-minute walk from our apartment in the 18th to a neighborhood café, called KB, located at the top of rue des Martyrs, in the 9th. Soon after we discovered it, it became our daily ritual to go there. We began showing up every morning at around 9 A.M., ordering the same thing (two hot lattes), and cheerfully saying hello to the two guys working behind the counter the same way every single time. And yet, even after going there for a full month, these same guys acted as if they had never seen us before and were indifferent and abrupt, no matter how smiley and American and friendly and *"bonjour-y"* we were.

Given that we knew no one in the city and just wanted to feel some sort of connection, we took their behavior toward us personally. Walking over each morning, we would warn each other not to react or be upset by their unwillingness to acknowledge us when we walked in, their decision to talk to each other for several minutes before even addressing us as we stood waiting to order, their interrupting us before our order was fully placed, their going back to their conversation and tuning us out as we tried to pay, or their looking around the café instead of at us as though we were not there—but still we were triggered every time.

On some mornings I would try and force an acknowledgment out of them by asking how they were with a robust, *"Ça va?"* (meaning, "How's it going?") when I stepped up to order. Rather than getting a warm and friendly, *"Ça va et vous?"* in return, which would be the normal American response, we were given a grunt and a shrug and an impatient *"Oui?"* ("Yes?") instead and handed a wooden number on a stick to take to the table to wait for our drinks. Not even a "got it" or "here you go," let alone a "thank you" in return.

It was humbling to start the day being treated so impersonally. It's not as if they didn't know who we were or what we wanted. We saw them every single day and ordered the exact same thing every time we came in. "How hard would it be to remember us?" we wondered under our breath.

It was enough to put us off for the entire morning. But the coffee, freshly baked cakes, fresh juice, and little breakfast paninis they served were so delicious, and the location was so prime, that we didn't want to go elsewhere in spite of feeling invisible.

Located on the square at the top of the charming rue des Martyrs, KB Café overlooked this quaint street filled with old-school fresh fruit and vegetable markets, fresh oyster and seafood vendors, great butchers and bakeries, cheese and chocolate shops, bookstalls and boutiques, some that had been there since the turn of the last century. It was the perfect place to shop for our daily fresh food, so we didn't want to let the impersonal greeting we received every morning at KB deter us from this area.

No, we would persist. Rather than being caught off guard each morning, we braced ourselves, determined not to take the less than enthusiastic welcome personally so we could enjoy their delicious wares. We even tried smothering them with cheery, chipper, smiley, American morning-greeting kindness, but it made no difference.

After a while it began to dawn on us that maybe being abrupt and not very warm to people was simply the Parisian baristas' game, and we just needed to learn how to play it. These guys treated everyone the same way, and no one but us seemed bothered in the least. The way other customers played the game was to be equally dismissive of them, talking to each other and making the barista wait for their order. Getting clear on that changed everything.

It also made me aware of my own inner turmoil and how as humans we all have to deal with some degree of imperfect connection all the time. Maybe these guys were just being themselves, and my unhappy state was just misinterpreting it all. Maybe they weren't really such bad guys, but I just felt they were because I wanted them to be nice to me and they weren't.

I also began to notice that we weren't the only regulars. Just as we did, other people came in every day with their books, their computers, their friends, or just alone, sitting and sipping coffees for as long as they wanted, no matter how many people stood in line waiting for a table. If you were sitting, it was not your concern who wasn't. It was more than okay to camp out for hours if you felt like it. And people did.

In America we would probably have been asked to move along if there was a long line waiting and we had finished our coffee. Here it was first come, first serve and every man for himself at the café. There was no "let's be sensitive to our fellow man" evident anywhere. Having been guilty of extreme overgiving, overcaring, overresponsibility, and oversensitivity all my life, I found it an adjustment getting used to. I realized that maybe I could use a little of this attitude myself. Given that my soul brought me here and I trusted that everything I was experiencing offered a gift in some way, maybe this more "centered-in-me" behavior could teach me a well-needed lesson and help me balance all that "energy out" with a little "energy in."

Another thing I noticed was that our French baristas were never in a rush to get to our—or anyone's—order, and often the line of customers backed up out the door. If you wanted to have a coffee here, you simply had to relax and wait a *long* time, and the customers seemed to know and accept this. With our ingrained "hurry up and get going" American way of being, slowing down and surrendering to this new pace and attitude took a lot of adjusting on our part.

At first it was so irritating it set me on edge, as I found myself coming face-to-face with perhaps my biggest character flaw—my extreme impatience—each and every time I walked in the door. I found myself tapping my toe, shifting from one leg to the other, jiggling my keys, sighing loudly, leaning forward and then back in the line, trying to get a move on, all to no avail. No one here seemed to be in a hurry to do any job. Ever.

In the end I realized that if I didn't take my foot off the mental gas pedal and slow down, I was going to blow a gasket. I surrendered, accepting that to enjoy living here at all, I either had to start my day three hours earlier if I wanted to accomplish all I had set out to do or cut my agenda in half and relax and smell the coffee.

KB Café was a local meeting place, where groups—especially of young people—hung out for hours, talking and smoking cigarettes around the small tables situated outside the café. It didn't matter that it was really cold outside. Everyone seemed immune to the cold and far more interested in having very loud, intense conversations, which sounded more like arguments and debates than the friendly banter I was used to hearing in America.

Although both Sabrina and I spoke adequate French, these rapid-fire conversations left us completely in the dark as to what they were saying or why they seemed so intense about it. We just shook our heads, feeling like outsiders, and realized we had a long way to go if we were to fully understand Parisians, let alone blend in.

"Bah, ouais!" Sabrina said, sounding just like the guys next to us. We laughed.

Shopping 101

Whether in rue des Martyrs or anywhere else in Paris, I later learned, shopping for food was sacred and never to be rushed. The biggest challenge was that food shopping was essentially new to me. While married, I was the writer, the teacher, the traveler, and the consultant, and Patrick stayed home and did all the cooking. He was actually fantastic at it, and dinner was a nearly nightly gourmet experience.

Luckily for me, Sabrina had the same talent and love for cooking as her father had, so she took the helm when it came to shopping for and preparing our meals. I tagged along, watching and learning from her, as well as from the other shoppers, enjoying this whole new creative world that I had avoided for all these years.

We both quickly learned there was a way to interact with the shopkeepers if you wanted the experience to go well. It was absolutely essential to greet them with a polite *"Bonjour, Monsieur* (or *Madame)"* upon entering the shop. To be remiss in saying *"Bonjour"* was considered the ultimate insult and was met with an icy stare and a wall of contempt that would send you running out the door, a lesson I learned on one of those early-in-the-game mornings when I was still foolishly trying to get a lot done before I started work just after noon. A lack of greeting is an egregious lack of manners, and the shopkeepers reserve the right to ice you out if you fail to be polite when entering *their* shop—and they will.

In America, greeting the shop owner or the people working there is not done as often, and in fact, sometimes shoppers consider it off-putting and intrusive when someone greets them at the door. We have far more of a "give me my space" attitude back home, but perhaps this is because in America we have so much space. Here in Paris, every tiny inch of the city is utilized, no shop wasting even a centimeter of their precious space, and life is much more up close and face-to-face, if not personal, here.

We also learned that in Paris people are very formal. You don't just say *"Bonjour,"* a friendly yet casual hello as we might back home. To say simply "Bonjour" is considered a lack of decency and civility, and just plain rude. You must say, "Bonjour, *Madame"* or "Bonjour, *Monsieur."* You are also expected to say *"Au revoir"* when leaving the shop, just as you would when leaving someone's home, which these shops often were, I came to find out, with the proprietor living upstairs or in the back.

I actually loved these polite exchanges. It felt good to be gracious and say hello in a proper way to everyone I met, as they did to me. And unlike the baristas in KB Café, most of the shopkeepers warmed *a little* once properly greeted. It was the beginning of some of our first relationships in Paris.

And that seemed to be a key difference from the U.S.—shopping in Paris was all about civil relationships. In America, food shopping often takes place in huge supermarkets, where you pick out everything quickly, throw it in a cart, and check out in a flash, hardly ever noticing anyone. Even in big cities such as New York, where shopping takes place in the neighborhood markets, you are still expected to help yourself, bring everything to the counter for a swift checkout, then quickly get on your way as there are others *waiting*.

On rue des Martyrs, food shopping is done in an entirely different way. For one, just as in the cafés, every customer entering a shop is absolutely unconcerned with the person behind him or her and could care less if that person has to wait all day. Shopkeepers indulge each customer with their full attention. Shoppers take their sweet time deciding what they want, asking questions, demanding samples, talking about the weather, asking about the shopkeeper's family and more as they *slowly* and determinedly make their choices. Food here is sacrosanct and not to be rushed, under any circumstance. Each purchase is made carefully, mindfully, with customers asking for the backstory on every product they purchase. Where is it from? When did it come in? What farm? What region? What family owned the farm? Did the family who once owned that farm keep it in the family, or did they sell it to another farmer, because if that's the case, they didn't want that particular piece of meat or fish or produce any longer. As I listened to the shoppers ahead of me, it felt as if these women—for most of them were women—were making inquiries about a potential *adoption* rather than simply buying groceries for dinner. All any person waiting in line behind the customer being served can do is relax and wait. At least we know that when our turn comes, we can take the same amount of time as the one before us did.

But, of course, we never did. First, we were far too insecure to take up that much attention, and second, Sabrina and I just didn't have that many questions. We were decisive shoppers. We pointed out what we wanted and got on our way, knowing that it would all be delicious and always far more fresh and tasty than the food we usually found back home, even in the organic food markets. Maybe it was the romance of the market; maybe it was the freshness of the produce, usually brought in straight from the farms or from the sea that morning; maybe it was the lengthy conversations we were privy to—who knows?—but everything we ate was simply and deeply and profoundly and incredibly delicious.

Another thing I quickly discovered on our steep shopping learning curve, at least on rue des Martyrs, is that self-service is a no-no. When entering a small shop, especially one of the small fruit-and-vegetable markets along the street, rather than reach out and take what you want, you must wait for the shopkeeper to arrive, then point out what you want when it is your turn and have the shopkeeper get it for you.

I learned this lesson painfully when I spontaneously reached out and took two apples from a beautifully stacked apple display one morning and immediately got screamed at. *"Ne touchez pas, Madame!"* ("Don't touch, Madame!") the shop owner cried, startling me so much that I dropped the apples and put my hands in the air. The shop owner then marched over, picked up the apples I had dropped, stuck them in my face, and accusingly asked if those were the ones I wanted. He carefully reorganized his now-disturbed display as he spoke, then turned back to me and said, *"Il faut demander,"* meaning, "You have to ask me to get things for you in this shop." I got it.

Embarrassed at having made such a terrible *faux pas,* I apologized profusely but was met with only a silent raised eyebrow in rebuke. At that point all I wanted to do was run away and remove myself from his ire, and did after paying for the apples, even though I would have loved to buy many more of his beautiful-looking fruits and vegetables.

It took several weeks for me to summon the courage to venture back in. Knowing the protocol now, however, I was prepared to do things the right way. Starting out with an enthusiastic, yet relaxed (or at least appearing to be relaxed), *"Bonjour, Monsieur. Comment allez-vous aujourd'hui?"* (meaning, "Good morning, sir, and how are you today?"). I waited anxiously to see if he would remember our last interaction. Fortunately, it was as if Monsieur Fruit Man had never encountered me before.

He was delightful and friendly and, since there were no other customers in the shop at the moment, highly accommodating and outright flirtatious with me as I pointed out all the things I wanted. He even stopped to offer me a fresh strawberry that had just come in that morning, then a slice of delicious papaya, and insisted that I try one of the green grapes plucked from the beautifully arranged bunch before me as he prepared my selections, plopping it directly into my mouth.

Admiring his shop as I waited, I fully appreciated what an artisan he was, and said so, which left him beaming with pride. Each stack of fruit and vegetables had been carefully arranged in such a loving and artistic way, I felt as though I were in the middle of a still life. I was completely entranced by the love and care he put into his shop and in me as I gathered up my packages and put them in my chariot.

We chatted about how he began his day at 5 A.M. to receive and arrange his produce before opening. He pointed out how he had to sort out his fruits and vegetables when they arrived, choosing to display and sell only the very best for his customers, as they would accept nothing less. *"Ah, non! Pas possible!"* he emphasized, assuring me his customers would rebel if his wares were anything substandard. This wasn't just his job. It was his devotion. I floated out of his shop feeling *served*. It was such a contrast to not feeling served at KB. Both were so *French!* This country was such a contradiction.

Out with the Old

Getting our bearings and making ourselves comfortable occupied the first few weeks, full-time. The days flew by, with me collapsing into bed, exhausted, every night around midnight.

Once my mind began to settle down, my anxiety kicked in. The truth was, being married was a major part of my identity, one that I now realized had been an anchor in my life. Now that my marriage was over, I needed to find a new anchor, one that wasn't attached to my relationship or my past.

Now I was free to fully anchor in the *exclusive* care and support of *me*, which I was shocked to realize I had never done in my entire life. I was always busy with the care and the support of those around me. I not only did this even as a child and all through my marriage, but also in my work as an intuitive consultant, teacher, and guide.

It was what I did because, *as a woman*, that was what I was taught to do, trained to do, expected to do, was good at doing, and truthfully mostly loved doing. My training just happened not to include caring for myself, and I wasn't even sure who the "me" was who now needed to be cared for.

I discovered that my private self, the Sonia who wasn't married, who wasn't raising children, who wasn't giving workshops or teaching or giving private consultations or helping friends, was shockingly fragile at the moment, and more than a little pissed off.

This private self, the part of me that wanted to feel secure and personally loved, *not* for what I did but for who I was intrinsically, had been ignored and neglected *by me* for most of my life. Underneath a lifetime dedicated to serving others, this part of me had been hiding, waiting, lonely, and invisible for as long as I could remember.

I could no longer deny this hidden self. This long-ignored side of me needed to be reckoned with and was not about to go away. It was time I saw and honored this banished part of myself.

At the same time, I also realized how all my life I had been trained to be self-reliant and strong, and strongly discouraged from asking much from others. I had been taught to be accommodating, resilient, and cheerful, a good womanly warrior who would bravely face my fears and help others with no complaint. It was what made me feel worthy.

While this warrior aspect had served me all my life and helped me fulfill my mission as an intuitive guide in a world that denied intuition even existed, it began to dawn on me that this wasn't ever a *natural* part of my essence. Or a healthy one. I had developed these warrior traits out of necessity, and was grateful for the strength they had afforded me. But they were exhausting habits and left me feeling depleted, isolated, and burned out.

If I had been more sensitive to me all along, instead of being angry that Patrick wasn't sensitive enough, would things have turned out differently? I wondered. Maybe I would have made different and kinder-to-me choices. Now it was too late to know.

All I knew now was that I was no longer inspired to be the warrior. I had no more "war" in me. It was over. All I wanted was to end all battles and find deep inner peace for the first time in my life.

I intuitively knew that Paris drew me because it was the embodiment of the sacred feminine for me. A place where I came to learn to be sensitive to me. It was time.

The city was unceasingly beautiful, both in architecture and way of life. From the gorgeous buildings to the exquisitely displayed wares to the attractive flower shops on every corner and flower boxes in every window to the delicious meals served in charming restaurants to the chic fashions to the elegant gardens, even down to the pampered pooches marching alongside people throughout the city—everywhere I looked, Paris was an aesthetic banquet that fed my soul. Paris was beauty, and I was bathing in her healing waters just being here.

It was a strange juxtaposition, because as sensuous as the city itself was, most Parisians I encountered were highly intellectual. In fact, they worship the God of reason and rarely consider listening to their spirit or following their intuition. I don't even think they have a proper word for one's "spirit," which is the source and voice of your intuition, and what I follow every day.

Perhaps we could help one another, I mused, as I marched up and down Paris, from one end to another, day after day. Paris had such a strong outer feminine identity, maybe it could help me build a new, more feminine one of my own. One that was as committed to my own grace and beauty and harmony as Paris was committed to hers. And I had such a strong intuition and inner voice guiding me that maybe I could help Parisians as well, one person and one encounter at a time, to open their hearts, find their own inner voice, and trust their intuition and the inner truth that they might be in search of.

Day by day, I slowly began to take the first steps toward letting go of my old caretaking identity and embracing a new self-caring one instead. There was an incredible freedom in being in a foreign and exotic city, where no one knew me or had any expectations of me and I was completely untethered from the past. I was now free to establish new priorities and make new, more educated, self-loving, self-aware, and, yes, self-centered (or, at least, centered in myself) choices.

The only question that faced me now was, who is "myself"? Even though I had walked not one but two pilgrimages across Spain to find healing, forgiveness, and acceptance, and had come to much resolution about the past, there remained that deeply hungry inner self. Stripped of all the layers of identity I had carried throughout my entire life, this raw, unformed, fragile, needy (to my horror), and undefended self now demanded my attention, love, care, and protection.

I was now being asked by my soul to become fully and uncompromisingly self-loving for the first time in my life. It had long been my prayer. Divorce was just how it had been painfully answered. By not being married, I was now free to focus on healing me. That was my gift in all of this. I was determined to accept it.

How to Be Parisian

As much as I loved being in Paris at the moment, I was still very much in the "flight" part of my "fight or flight" reaction to the divorce. Having plowed through the divorce as fast as I did, everything in me was still racing, and every day I felt as if I had to get up and go, almost as though in a panic. I was still running. Although in reality I had nowhere to run to.

This was especially evident on Sundays in Paris, which both Sabrina and I had come to *really* dislike. It could have been the relentless, cold, gray hue of the Paris winter that permeated everything and the fact that so many places were closed on Sundays, because Sundays were family days and everyone was at home enjoying dinner and family time together. The truth was we simply felt left out. So we did what we always did when we were uncomfortable: we bundled up and went for a walk.

Apart from rue des Martyrs, which was open on Sunday mornings and closed on Mondays, and Montmartre, which was packed with tourists and a hassle to visit on Sundays, the areas around our apartment closed up tight as a drum, and Paris became a ghost town.

One particular Sunday morning, in a full-on feeling-left-out-on-a-Sunday gray funk, we decided we would go to the Louvre and then follow up with a late lunch/early dinner at one of our favorite cafés, Café Marly, located on the plaza in front of the museum, overlooking the famous pyramid entrance.

Rushing to get out the door and escape our discomfort, we bundled up in our winter coats, hats, and gloves and stepped out. Halfway down the stairs, I realized I had left my wallet in the apartment and quickly turned and ran back to get it. Sabrina waited a few steps ahead, and I raced to catch up. Suddenly, my feet slipped on the polished stairs and flew right out from underneath me.

Screaming and attempting to grab the rail to keep from falling, I spun around and somehow ended up on my stomach, hands in front, trying to catch my fall, pointing headfirst down the stairs and still traveling.

My waterproof winter coat was so slick on the already extremely slippery stairs, that I continued to slide as if on a luge, picking up speed as I went, screaming the entire way. I flew right past Sabrina, who also screamed, at which point the neighbors on all the floors rushed out of their apartments, demanding to know what the unholy commotion was.

I continued sliding down the round staircase until I shot out on the *rez de chaussée* and hit the front door with my head. Sabrina, along with all the neighbors, came running after me, but I just couldn't face them. Instead, I jumped up and ran out the door as fast as lightning because I didn't want anyone to see my face. The humiliation would have been unbearable. I could faintly hear Sabrina following behind, yelling, "Mom, wait! Stop! Are you okay?"

I kept running all the way to the corner and around it before I finally stopped. I felt really banged up and bruised, but my ego had taken the worst beating of all. Sabrina finally caught up, gasping, "Oh my God! Mom—what happened? How did you end up flying down the stairs like that? Are you okay?"

Still reeling from the whole experience, I brushed off my coat and looked at her. "Yes. I'm okay."

Trying desperately to look concerned, Sabrina suddenly burst out laughing and couldn't stop. At first I was insulted and tried to tell her I was hurt, but she was too hysterical to hear me, so I gave up.

What had just happened was so ridiculous that I started laughing as well. It was useless to try and gain any sympathy. I gave up. "Let's keep walking. I have to regain my composure and dignity."

Fortunately, I *was* okay. We kept laughing all the way to the Louvre, Sabrina recounting, over and over, the shocked look on the neighbors' faces as she tried to explain that her mother had just flown headfirst past her down the stairs.

Feeling somewhat grateful for the good laugh, even if it was at my own expense, I couldn't help but recognize how my headfirst flight down the stairs revealed just how painfully ungrounded and out of control I really was right now. It was humbling to find myself in such a literal free fall.

This lesson in slip-sliding away was not lost on me. Realizing, as always, how the outside mirrors the inside, I could at least *appreciate* how following my spirit meant at times I just had to put my head down and keep going, even if it did mean losing control and getting a little banged up along the way.

After all, following your spirit is not about staying in control and avoiding pain in life. It's about surrendering control and meeting life head-on. I just needed to slow down and stop running so I didn't do it at 90 miles an hour.

The walk to the Louvre was calming as I mentally surrendered to my present inner state, as out of control as it was. We wandered through three or four galleries before deciding we were hungry, then walked over to Café Marly and settled in on the terrace. Even though it was freezing outside, there were warming lamps between the tables, allowing us to sit outside as we had our lunch. Needing to soothe my battered soul, we enjoyed a beautiful meal, accompanied by glasses of champagne, which hit the spot.

As we ate, we talked about the Sunday blues and how to handle them. Sundays were the days we felt most like outsiders, voyeurs—allowed to look but not to enter the heart of Paris. While we temporarily lived there, we knew that we were far from belonging. In fact, we felt as though we didn't belong anywhere, which—after having had such deep roots at home—was a painful and scary feeling. After a second glass of champagne, I decided I wasn't going to let those feelings take over. Suddenly, I had a mission: I was determined to belong.

The next day, the first thing I did was pick up a brand-new book called *How to Be Parisian* at the English bookstore on rue de Rivoli. It was written by a group of chic French women who felt it was their duty to teach the rest of us how to step up our game.

In it were lots of tips on how to dress, act, speak, behave with friends, cook, and even drink champagne properly (with ice cubes, apparently, because otherwise it gives you bad breath—though I wondered if that might not be more from the cigarettes so many "cool" French women smoked along with their glasses of champagne).

Feeling absolutely confused about who I was at the moment, becoming "Parisian" seemed highly appealing. *After all, what is more chic, more cool, more feminine than being Parisian?* I thought, seeking to restore my presently trashed self-esteem.

Manual in hand, the first instruction I took to heart was to get my Parisian uniform together: a button-down white shirt and a black blazer, two things I have never worn in my life.

I embarked on a mission to find the perfect white shirt. My first stop was Galeries Lafayette, the upscale and very chic department store located at the bottom of the hill where our walks seemed to spill out naturally day after day.

Galeries Lafayette is a beautiful five-story art nouveau oasis of Parisian elegance and sophistication housed under a magnificent stained-glass dome ceiling just behind the Opéra in the center of Paris. The minute you step in, you are transported into another world, one that is the epitome of elegance, filled to the brim with the finest designer goods that Paris—and the world—has to offer.

Inside were mini boutiques for each top designer: Prada, Gucci, Yves Saint Laurent, Chanel, Givenchy, Versace, Dior, Sonia Rykiel, Fendi, and all the other top names in fashion. This would be the perfect place to find my mandatory white shirt.

Wandering from designer to designer, I finally found the perfect shirt in one of the French boutiques on the third floor. It was classic white, stiff-collared, button-down, and *très* expensive for what it was. Just what the book called for. Motivated by my current insecurity and my habitual impulsiveness, I didn't hesitate to buy it. I slammed down the 100 euros without blinking an eye, even though that was a crazy price for a basic white shirt, pleased with my find and feeling more confident now that I was well on my way to embodying my new "Parisian" persona.

I marched straight home to show Sabrina my find, fully expecting applause and an exuberant, "Bravo!"

Instead, when I put it on, Sabrina rolled her eyes at me and said, "You look like an office worker. Where in the hell are you going to wear that?"

Demoralized by her frank assessment, I fought for this new version of me. "Just wait," I said. "I haven't found the black blazer yet."

"When have you ever worn a black blazer, Mom? You will look ridiculous in one."

"No, I won't," I insisted. "You'll just have to get used to my Paris look."

That night we planned to go out to dinner and I decided I would wear my new shirt in spite of Sabrina's comment, even if I did not yet have the mandatory black blazer to go with it. I put it back on and buttoned it up. It felt stiff. I tucked it into my jeans. It looked stupid. I pulled it out of my jeans and let it hang loose and unbuttoned a few buttons. It looked sloppy. I sat down and put on my shoes and it crawled up my back. I stood up and pulled it down once again but I felt like I was in a straitjacket. I tore it off and threw it in the corner. Sabrina was right. It was not me at all. I pulled out my favorite blue pullover sweater and put it on. "Ahh. Relief."

I walked into the living room and said to Sabrina, "I'm ready to go."

"Where's your white shirt?" she asked. "I thought you were going to wear it tonight and make your new 'Parisian' debut?"

"It was too uncomfortable to wear," I admitted.

"I told you so." She laughed.

As I went to sleep later that night, I thought about the champagne I'd ordered, *with ice cubes. At least I don't have bad breath,* I thought with a sigh of relief. *That's a start anyway.*

Red Lipstick

In spite of the white shirt disaster, the next night I found myself sneaking back to the book to get more tips on attaining "Parisienne cool." The next instruction that caught my eye was to wear bright red lipstick and little other makeup.

That I could do. I liked red lipstick and had worn it from time to time over the years, although not lately. A stylish friend of mine who worked in advertising in New York told me a few years earlier that women of a "certain age" shouldn't wear red lipstick, as it made them look older. Then he strongly hinted that I was fast approaching that "certain age."

That was such an American attitude. Getting older is the last thing a woman is ever to do in the U.S. We have to stay young looking no matter what if we want to be treated as relevant. Older women have no place in American culture. Ours is a culture that worships youth. And as I was "older," I succumbed to his admonition and gave up the red lipstick.

After reading this red-lipstick tip in the book, however, I began looking around Paris (where older women are revered and respected) to see if there was a similar stigma here. I was thrilled to see there was not. Older women everywhere had on red lipstick, and they looked just beautiful and wore it with pride. Another reason to love Paris—at least here I didn't have to face that unspoken judgment over age. I could be comfortable with my age and not feel dismissed or overlooked as I might have been at home. As with their wine and cheese, French people considered aging an improvement. It was so refreshing.

Reassured about the red, I marched back to the Galeries Lafayette and straight to the cosmetics department on the first floor, which was vast. There were gorgeous makeup counters everywhere, and elegant saleswomen of all ages floated in between, spray bottles of perfume in hand, offering spritzes and assistance at the same time. They swarmed down upon me like buzzards going in for the kill, smiling and saying, *"Bonjour, Madame.* May I help you?" In English, I might add.

Do I look that American? I wondered, not having even opened my mouth. *How do they know not to speak to me in French?* I sunk further into insecurity. *I must be more obvious than I thought I was. I should have worn my white shirt*, I thought. This revelation made me all the more determined to get the red lipstick and slather it on right then and there.

The rows and rows of makeup counters before me made it difficult to know where to begin my search. They were all so beautiful, and the saleswomen all so elegant—if slightly intimidating—that I just wandered around for a while.

Finally, I decided on Chanel. It was familiar. And what was more quintessentially Paris than Chanel, after all? I approached the counter. Looking at the display, I could see they had lots of red lipsticks. In fact, the *entire* lipstick display was made of red lipsticks. There was cherry red, red-red, blue-red, orange-red, clear red, dark brown red, almost purple-blue red, and more to choose from.

I had only a moment to open a few and look at them before the saleswoman pounced on me, saying, *"Bonjour, Madame,* how may I assist you today?" in *English.*

"Bonjour, Madame," I replied. "I am looking for a red lipstick."

"Ahh. Très bien," she said, nodding in approval. "Any particular red?" she asked, which struck me as slightly silly. How many women come in saying, I am looking for a particular red lipstick, a blue-red with tinges of orange, perhaps? But then again, this was Paris. Of course the women here would have a *particular* red lipstick in mind.

They were some of the most *particular* creatures I had ever observed. They probably knew exactly which red lipstick they wanted and asked for it by name. "I want the Heroic Red lipstick by Givenchy," or "I want Red 999 by Dior," or "Absolu Rouge by Lancôme."

I looked at two or three reds on display as the saleswoman stared straight at me with a frozen smile, not giving me an inch of space to explore the offerings in private, before I succumbed to the pressure I felt. Pointing to 2 of the 10 lipsticks on display, I said, "I'll take these two," not really sure what color they were.

"Parfait, Madame," the saleswoman said. "Can I show you anything else today?"

"No, nothing. *Merci, Madame,"* I said, wanting to pay and leave as fast as I could. Meanwhile, the saleslady *slowly* wrapped the lipsticks with the utmost care and delicacy—with tissue paper and ribbons—and then placed them in a small box, then a small bag, and handed them to me, as if they were Baccarat crystal goblets.

I handed her my credit card, which she processed. Then she asked me for my *"petite"* signature, which made me smile. Parisians love for things to be *"petit,"* as opposed to Americans, who like things to be big.

I heard them referring to things this way often. *Une petite signature. Un petit moment. Un petit dessert* at the restaurant. *Un petit echantillon,* which meant a sample of something; *une petite amuse-bouche,* a little taste treat served before a main meal at a restaurant. Maybe they did things in a *petit* way to make life more manageable. One *petit* step at a time, for example.

I grasped my *petit paquet* after signing my receipt and walked out. "I'll feel better when I have on un *petit* lipstick," I told myself. "More Parisian. No one will speak English to me then."

Or at least I hoped so.

The truth was that I was simply out of sorts and not at all comfortable in my own skin these days.

How could this happen? I wondered. *I am a world-class spiritual teacher and writer, respected by thousands and great at what I do. Why all of a sudden am I trying to dress myself up in Parisian costumes and red lipsticks, trying to fit in?*

But just as I thought this, I realized that was exactly *what* I was trying to do: to fit in, to feel as though I belonged and wasn't just a voyeur wandering around like a lost puppy. I didn't want just to live in Paris, I wanted Parisians to *like* me, to accept—even to love—me, and I was hoping it would help if I looked more like them.

"Just relax, Sonia," I reassured myself on the way back up the hill to the apartment. "Enjoy your *petit* lipstick and give yourself a *petit moment* to fit in. It takes a while to belong, to be accepted, and you must be patient. It'll come."

Hot Tempers

At times we had to go to the Carrefour market just down the hill on rue de Clignancourt for some of our basic household supplies and groceries, like olive oil and milk. We had to check our chariot with a store guard before we were allowed into the store. Maybe they thought we would load it up and steal things otherwise. Who knows?

It was best to get there in the morning because shopping there at night was pure chaos. But, of course, there were days when we didn't make it, so we went after work, around 7 P.M.

There were so many customers at that hour that it was difficult to move from aisle to aisle, and the checkout line usually stretched all the way to the back of the store. And, of course, it moved very *slowly*. An evening trip to Carrefour took a long time, although it was only five minutes from our front door.

Once inside, in spite of the crowd, I loved the colorful cast of characters surrounding me. It was a United Nations experience, and I felt as though I were at an international airport on a weekend as I strolled through the aisles, getting what we needed.

Most of the people we saw didn't look very happy, however, and sometimes tensions flared. Once, while near the front of the checkout line, we suddenly heard a commotion. The next thing we knew, there was a full-on brawl going on in the street just outside the store. It started with two guys arguing loudly, but within five seconds, others felt the need to chime in. Soon there were more than 30 men involved, at first just yelling at each other.

Then one guy got so worked up he pushed the other, and that started a frenzy.

Both fascinated and scared, we watched through the window from our ringside seat close to the cashier as the melee ignited in a flash. Both men and women alike began shoving and screaming, and for a second, it seemed like a riot was about to unfold. People entering the store turned around and ran outside to join in. Although I was holding my breath as I watched, mesmerized, the cashier didn't even turn her head to look up and just kept on ringing up groceries. Obviously this was nothing new as far as she was concerned.

Seconds later those who thought of themselves as peacekeepers jumped in and started to pull the fighters apart, yelling for everyone to calm down and go home. The entertainment was over and the crowd dispersed as fast as it had gathered. The entire thing flared up and died down by the time it was our turn to check out. Both Sabrina and I were relieved. By the time we had freed our chariot from house arrest with the store guard and placed our purchases inside, the street was calm.

The Laundromat

One of the most freeing aspects of living in the Old Lady was learning just how simply I could live. In Chicago, I owned a three-story Victorian home that required endless maintenance, each floor full of stuff, and a car that constantly needed gas and insurance, all of it taking up a lot of mental space.

So many luxurious creature comforts back home, like the big 10-cycle washer and dryer I had owned, now seemed obscene and unnecessary. Here, in the Old Lady, we had the tiniest little clothes washer ever, but it did the job—although for the life of me I could never understand why it had to run for almost two hours each time we used it. *What on earth could possibly require such an industrial-strength cleanse?* I wondered, praying our clothes would come out in one piece and not shredded into ribbons from such an enthusiastic once-over every time I started a load.

Given the lengthy workout each wash load went through, we soon realized that this just meant we had to wash our clothes less often. At home I threw things into the wash without thinking. Here I was more mindful. Washing clothes that often was wasting water, so I was fine with doing laundry less frequently. It made me feel better to have a reduced carbon footprint.

Drying the clothes was another matter altogether. There was no dryer in the Old Lady. Our clothes had to be hung up on a drying rack and left to dry, ending up stiff and crunchy from all the limestone and minerals in the water. That wasn't as much of a problem as the drying time needed, given that the apartment was so cold. It could take up to a day or two for some things to be fully dry, especially our jeans.

Since the drying rack was so tiny, I had to find other places to hang the clothes. I laid them on the dining-room table. I hung them over the backs of the dining-room chairs. I hung them over the shower door and draped them across the cubicles in the entry-way that we used for our closet.

One day while Sabrina was working on the phone, I had the rest of the day off, so I did the laundry. When the wash was done, I took the clothes out and began to hang them to dry as quietly and creatively as I could.

Among the things that had been washed was Sabrina's new cozy robe, which she had purchased a few weeks earlier. Since her robe took up all the space on the drying rack, I looked around for another place to hang it up, and without thinking, I tossed it over the standing LED lamp just behind me. I turned my back to put a few other things out to dry, when I simultaneously smelled something burning and heard Sabrina shouting to her client, "Oh my gosh—I have to call you back. My mom just set my robe on fire!"

Just as I turned around, the smoldering robe went up in flames. The exposed LED lightbulb burned a hole in the acrylic robe in a matter of seconds, and the fire was rapidly spreading to the rest of the robe.

As I grabbed the robe off the light, Sabrina ran past me toward the shower, screaming, "Hurry, throw it in here!"

I couldn't believe how fast everything happened.

"Mom, you almost burned the apartment down!" Sabrina cried as she watched the flames die down under the showerhead, understandably upset.

"I know," I said, "I can't believe it. Thank God I didn't. That would have been awful."

"Yes, it would have been," she snapped, marching back to the dining room. "Now if you don't mind, I have to call my client back. We need to open the windows. The apartment smells like burning chemicals."

I apologized profusely. "I am so sorry, Sabrina. I'll get you another robe tomorrow. Who knew it was made of plastic?"

When she called her client back, I overheard her saying, while laughing, "I'm so sorry. My mom just accidentally set my robe on fire."

Then a moment later, "No, we're okay. I just need to keep an eye on her."

I never made that mistake again.

Washing our sheets and towels in the little washer was a very bad idea. It took at least a full day for them to dry out, if not more, and in spite of the nearly two-hour tour in the washer, they never seemed quite fresh in the end. So I decided to look for a laundromat in the neighborhood instead. It would just be simpler.

After scouting around, I found one down the hill from our apartment in the other direction, just across from the Château d'Eau métro stop. When I entered, I learned from the Moroccan woman who worked there that it was not very expensive to drop off my laundry and have it washed, dried, ironed, and folded. She pointed out the prices listed on a sign on the wall.

Delighted to no end to have discovered this little luxury, I immediately went home and packed up all the sheets, towels, and our comforters and walked them back.

When I returned to the laundromat, the Moroccan woman I had spoken with earlier was out to lunch, and someone I assumed was her son took my bundle. I asked him how long it would take to get it back, and he mumbled something I couldn't quite make out. I thought he said that night, so I repeated in French, *"Çe soir?"* meaning, "Tonight?" He sort of nodded his head as he carelessly took my large bundle and tossed it on the pile of clothes behind him. I repeated, *"À çe soir, alors,"* meaning, "I'll see you tonight." He didn't say a word as he handed me my ticket.

After work, at 7 P.M., I headed down the hill, eager to pick up my freshly washed laundry, thinking about what a good night's sleep I would have in my crisp, clean, ironed sheets.

When I got there, however, the young man was nowhere to be found, and the Moroccan woman I had spoken with in the morning was back. When I gave her my ticket and asked for the laundry, she shook her head and told me it would be another week before it would be finished.

"A week! That's not possible. The man who took my laundry earlier said it would be ready tonight." She shook her head again and said he didn't actually work there. He was just watching the place while she went to eat lunch. What he said was wrong, she explained, and she had no idea why he said it. Getting my laundry back today was not possible, and a week from today was the soonest it would be ready. Apparently everyone in the neighborhood brought their bedding to be washed, having the same problem doing it at home as I did, so there was a lot of laundry to be done. It was normal to take a week, or even more, to get it back, she explained, as though that should have been completely obvious to me.

Shocked that I had just checked out all our bedding and towels into laundry prison, I begged her either to give them back unwashed or allow me to pay more money to hurry up their return.

"We need them for tonight," I pleaded. "We have no more sheets and comforters."

Shaking her head once again, she said that my laundry was not on the premises and that it had been sent out to their other location for cleaning. It was long gone and that was that.

I continued to plead and she eventually took mercy on me and made a phone call. After a *very* long discussion in Arabic with someone on the other end of the phone, she finally hung up and told me my laundry would be ready tomorrow night. But I had to pay 30 euros more. That was a lot, but the apartment was freezing and we needed the comforters, so I agreed, grateful that we would have to sleep only one night without them. Not looking forward to telling Sabrina we had no sheets and comforters for the night, especially since I had just burned her robe the day before, I thought about offering to stay at a hotel for the night to make up for it.

I was grateful that she was a good sport about it when she received the news.

"So we have no sheets and blankets or comforters?" she asked. "And, of course, I have no robe. So what do we sleep in or on?"

"Our coats," I answered. "It's only one night. We can sleep in our clothes and coats. We'll be fine. Or we can go to a hotel."

"No, that's a hassle, although it's very tempting. It'll be too expensive. Let's just make it work," she said, invoking our motto these days.

"Thanks, Sabrina. Let me take you out to dinner. My treat."

She gladly accepted, as she was the cook, so we bundled up and once again set out the door.

Around the corner from our apartment and a few blocks into chic bohemian territory was a cool '50s-themed restaurant called *Le Cheri Bibi.* It was a hip little place featuring a lounge with sofas and a great signature zinc bar at the front and tables in the back, usually packed with nouveau beatniks and cool cats, and always requiring a reservation. Nonetheless, we thought we would try to get a table anyway as we walked by in search of food.

The restaurant opened at 7 P.M. but was rarely full until almost 8:30. Since it was just after 7 and empty, we walked in. "Let's just tell them we are Americans and that we eat fast," I said, "and see if they give us a table."

It worked. We were told that *normally* we could not be seated without a reservation, but if we did not stay too long, they would accommodate us. Thrilled, we plopped down and ordered two glasses of champagne (with ice cubes, of course) straight away.

The menu was fantastic: stuffed peppers with cheese, a huge farm-raised chicken with homemade fries and root vegetables for two, creative fresh salads of every sort, steaks and mashed potatoes, fresh salmon, and more. The best part was that it felt as if we were in someone's home and that Grandma was cooking in the kitchen. The food was so delicious it knocked us out.

We actually ended up staying longer than we had promised, as it was such a great place and the food didn't come out that fast, but no one ever came over to hurry us out.

We toasted to the fact that we were needing less and less to be comfortable, including sheets and blankets, and how liberating it felt. Then we walked home with our arms linked together, laughing all the way.

Falling asleep, wrapped in my coat that night, I realized how grateful I was to the Moroccan woman for her willingness to get my sheets and comforters back by tomorrow, as it clearly was no small feat.

While at first she was resistant, she eventually saw my distress and changed her mind. Though it was a simple matter, in the end, her willingness to help me meant a lot.

I made a note of that and decided that even though I was in an "it's all about me" phase of life, I would absolutely never shut the door to others in need. That was me being me, and I would preserve and protect this part of my nature no matter what. The trick was simply to find the balance between serving others and taking care of myself. Too tired to think any longer, I asked my guides to keep me on track and trusted they would. Then I fell asleep.

A Crisis of the Liver

Perhaps because I was in such need of internal care upon escaping to Paris, some of my favorite places to visit on our daily outings were French pharmacies. Unlike the pharmacies in America, which are often located at the back of supermarkets and mostly dedicated to the dispensing of medication, pharmacies here were an oasis of comfort, catering to a person's, and especially a woman's, soul. At least that's what it felt like to me

In them you could find what seemed like every single product invented to soothe and nurture and beautify your body from head to toe. My local pharmacy on rue des Martyrs embodied this ideal, and I stopped there every time we walked down the street, even if I didn't need a thing. Walking through the store was fun. Upon entering, on the left side of the store, all along the wall, was every type of hair-care product imaginable. There were shampoos and conditioners and hair masques and hairsprays, as well as hair supplements and vitamins to make your hair thicker, curlier, more moisturized, stronger, free of dandruff, more full of body, and simply more beautiful.

Next to the hair-care products were the skin-care products, with even more to offer than the hair-care section, though it was hard to believe that was possible. French women learn to take care of their skin at a very young age, and it becomes a central routine in every woman's life. So no wonder there were so many products to choose from to cleanse and moisturize to keep your skin young and glowing forever. Every single woman here used them.

Because I am an optimist at heart, I believed every word written on every box or bottle. After all, the French were the masters of feminine beauty. They knew what they were talking about.

"Look, Sabrina," I said, pointing to a new line of facial products made from grapes that had just arrived in the store that day, according to the sales rep standing near them. "It says here that this product has ingredients in it that keep grapes from shriveling up." I held up the brochure next to the display. "Because of that, this cream will keep my skin from shriveling up as well. How great is that? I need to get this."

"Mom, nothing but eating grapes keeps them from shriveling up," Sabrina retorted as she looked over the shelves herself. "But get it if you want to."

I ignored her and put both the day *and* night *crèmes* into my basket. Despite her skepticism, Sabrina had put just as many skin products into her basket as I had.

"So what are you getting?" I asked her. She enthusiastically showed me her new moisturizing cleanser, skin toner, and eye cream, as well as a lip balm and moisturizing facial mask she could place over her entire face, made of jellied hyaluronic acid.

"I need this," she said, just in case I might challenge her. "The water here makes my skin so dry."

Rather than challenge her, I wholeheartedly agreed it was a good idea and put one in my basket, as well. Whether the water was drying or not, these products nurtured our aching and dehydrated souls.

Along the wall on the other side of the store and at the front was a large section with every type of foot-care product imaginable. There were callous creams, Band-Aids, bunion socks, toenail clippers, heel pumices, files, and every remedy under the sun for what might ail one's feet. Having walked two 800-kilometer pilgrimages in the past two years, and nearly 20 kilometers a day since arriving in Paris, this section was my little slice of heaven.

Every time I entered the pharmacy, I found myself looking at all the ways to soothe my feet. It didn't take long to realize that I was drawn here for more than the foot relief. I kept returning for the promise of feeling more grounded, which this section suggested. Too bad this epiphany hadn't come *before* I had acquired so many foot-care products that I could have probably soothed the soles of the entire French soccer team at the end of its season.

Next to the foot-care section was the body-care section, containing scented soaps and body washes, scrubs, lotions, and "spritzes" in every scent on earth. There were milk baths, mud baths, sea salt baths, bubble baths, moisturizing baths, and exfoliating baths. There were also loofah mitts, body scrubbers, and back scrubbers to use in the baths.

After that section was an entire department devoted to hand care. In this area were nail polishes, hand lotions, cuticle creams, moisturizing gloves to wear while you slept, and every hand-care tool ever made. Just looking at these exotic products, I needed a moment.

In the center of the store were over-the-counter remedies for every possible ailment, including homeopathic and natural organic remedies. There were shelves of flower essences, aromatherapy oils, and all kinds of vitamins and supplements with such compelling promises of rejuvenation that I tossed a few of these into my basket every time, as well.

Of course, we had similar products in our American drugstores, but they weren't as glamorous as these products. The advertising and packaging that went along with the products were so convincing, so alluring, and the products so different and new and so *French,* that they felt much more appealing than the same thing back home.

In my imagination, it would take only a lather of silky shampoo, some shrivel-proof face cream, a nighttime spent with moisturizing gloves, a whiff of aromatherapy, a few passes of a loofah across my butt and a callus remover across my heels, and I would be scrubbed down, smoothed over, and restored to my premarriage self. I would be as good as new. Or, at the very least, these products would remove the shell-shocked look I feared I so clearly wore on my face these days. I hoped they would, anyway. And my very full basket confirmed that.

I wasn't the only one looking for relief in these spaces. The store was packed with people every single time we went in. By the huge number of pharmacies in Paris, I surmised that French people must be in just as much need of soul-soothing relief as I was. On our nightly walks, it seemed as though there was a pharmacy every 30 feet. Sometimes there would be two or three on one block, and during the day they would all be full.

As at the greengrocer, the French stood patiently in line (of course), waiting for the pharmacist to give them his or her full, unhurried attention. The pharmacist, intensely engaged and dedicated to bringing about his or her customers' relief, would listen patiently to every detail of their complaints, ask questions, answer questions, and offer suggestion upon suggestion. Their attention went far and beyond what I had ever experienced back in Chicago with any pharmacist (or doctor, for that matter) I had ever asked for advice when I had an ache or pain. And way beyond what I would ever *expect* from any pharmacist back home. Like most things in the U.S., conversations with doctors or pharmacists were mostly rushed encounters because others were *waiting*. We accepted that, as we didn't like to be kept waiting either. The difference here took some getting used to.

I know because I had to stand in line and listen to these people every time I had to check out. Sometimes I waited *20* minutes or more while the person or people ahead of me described their symptoms, asked questions, and discussed possible treatments with the pharmacist.

Having already surrendered to the waiting game, I used this time both to study the people and to learn more French. I learned how to say "backache," "bellyache," "leg cramps," "sinus problems," "toothache," "insomnia," "earache," and, my favorite, *crise de foie*, or "crisis of the liver." I believe it means a bellyache that comes from overeating and drinking the night before, which taxes both the stomach and liver, but I prefer to think of it as a full-blown liver crisis.

Metaphysical studies have taught me that the liver is the seat of emotion, so a "liver crisis," in my mind, at least, was in fact an emotional crisis. I so wanted to walk up to the pharmacist and tell her that I, too, had a *crise de foie,* but I knew I would probably get a fizzy bicarbonate of soda and a good burp instead of any real emotional relief.

Listening to these people as the weeks went by, I became convinced that the pharmacists in this country were some of the kindest, most loving people here. They showed endless patience with each person and were so helpful that I wondered if that was half the reason people lined up to speak to them as they did. I wished a pharmacist could wipe away my heartache and confusion with a suppository (the drug delivery method of choice, it seemed, given how many I saw handed out while standing in line all those hours). Wouldn't that be nice!

Unfortunately I had to work out my soul's aches and pains the normal way: through acceptance, forgiveness, faith, prayer, patience, self-loving choices, and time. *Well, at least my feet won't hurt and I'll have smooth, non-shriveled skin on the outside while I work on the inside.* It was something to be grateful for.

Why is it, I wondered, slathering on my fabulous foot cream that night, *that intellectually recognizing self-defeating patterns isn't enough to change them?* I knew, for example, that I had to love myself, and I did. Still there were those stubborn self-sabotaging behaviors that clung on like mold in the basement, and I had to work hard to scrape them off my bones.

Like working too hard, I thought, *instead of listening to my need for rest and not overdoing it.* It was just one of those stubborn patterns I learned in Catholic school, where I was applauded for being such a "good, hardworking girl."

Putting on my new French clay face mask, I suddenly realized that *not* working hard was a national priority here in France. In fact, the French have more vacation days than any other Europeans do. I laughed out loud as I realized that my work ethic would *never* be applauded here. If anything, I would be considered crazy for working as hard as I did. *Yet another very good reason my soul led me here,* I told myself, reassured by this little revelation that I was following some sort of soul-improvement plan. *Time to take it easy, Sonia.* Turning off the light, I decided I would relax tomorrow and not work at all. Then I fell asleep.

Daily Prayers
and Rituals

The day after arriving at the Old Lady, we set about creating an altar in the apartment, an absolute must in our home. We placed ours in the middle of the long stone dining-room table. It started with a few images and statues we had brought from home, but over time our altar began to grow and spread out until soon it took up almost the entire table.

On it were the many votive candles we retrieved from the churches we visited all over Paris, including Notre Dame, the Madeleine, Sacré-Cœur, and all the tiny neighborhood churches we passed by and visited on our daily walks.

We also placed on it scented candles from Galeries Lafayette (lots of those, given the pigeons) and holy cards and statues of the Mother Mary, Mary Magdalene, and Saint Theresa we had collected over the years, as they were the providers of feminine strength and nurturing comfort to whom we prayed for emotional healing.

On our altar were also images of our favorite feminine Hindu deities, picked up on our many trips to India, which we also brought along with us. These included Lakshmi, the goddess of abundance (I needed all the help from her I could get); Durga, the goddess who alleviates suffering (she worked alongside Mother Mary, Mary Magdalene, and Saint Theresa); and Kali, the goddess of death and destruction and the one who liberates you and brings you freedom once you face your fears. I was sure Kali was in service to my soul's growth in all of this. Still, ouch!

Also sitting on our altar was a small statue of Quan Yin, the goddess of compassion, which I had carried with me for years. I knew in my heart and soul that finding compassion for both me and my now ex-husband was the only way I was going to find peace in the end.

Every day we added something new to the altar to keep it feeling fresh and active. On some days we sprinkled newly dropped petals around our altar from the flowers we had bought. On other days we added bowls of fresh water and a newly lighted scented candle. On some days we placed candy and chocolates, as an offering of sweetness, or burned a stick of incense in gratitude for the help we were receiving.

We took care of the altar, often rearranging it, speaking lovingly and gratefully to our divine helpers, whom we felt were right there in the room with us, thanking them for their help. Our altar was a living altar and an active place in our apartment. Mother Mary, Mary Magdalene, Saint Theresa, Quan Yin, and our Hindu goddesses were our roommates as far as we were concerned, and we were happy to have them on board. They gave us strength and were good company, lifting us up and keeping us optimistic and free from fear of the unknown. With their help, we were beginning to slowly regain some confidence.

Our early mornings were spent in meditation and prayer. We sat quietly and focused inward for a while before doing anything else, including speaking to one another, quieting our minds and calling on the inner resources we needed to meet the day with an open heart, not burdened by the wounds of the recent past.

As we got going, jumping in and quickly out of the ice-bucket shower, we played beautiful music. First was a clearing mantra called the Gayatri mantra, beautifully sung by a German woman named Deva Premal, which cleared away all negative energy both within and around us and called in peace and love in its place.

We followed the Gayatri with "Little Bird" by Annie Lennox. With its lyrics about being lost and learning to lay down our burdens and fly away, this felt like the perfect theme song for us. It got us up, focused, in a good mood, and out the door, singing and dancing.

In no time life became a series of daily rituals. First prayer and meditation. Then shower and dress to Gayatri and dance to "Little Bird." On to KB Café and rue des Martyrs for shopping. Back for work, then out for long nightly walks after dinner. Then prayers again before passing out for the night.

Sometimes our mornings started with a visit to Sacré-Cœur instead of KB Café, especially on the weekends when the café was simply too crowded to bother with.

In spite of my distaste for the patriarchal Catholic Church ideology and male oppression in general at the moment, I still loved Catholic churches themselves and their rituals, and this was one of my favorites. It was dedicated to the Sacred Heart of Jesus and his love for humanity. More than anything, I needed to feel that love right now and did every time I walked in.

Upon entering we were met with the most beautiful mosaic on the ceiling—one of the largest mosaics in the world. Here was the risen Christ dressed all in white (as opposed to the dying Christ on the Cross) with his arms extended, revealing a golden heart, surrounded by adorers and saints and angels. This mosaic provided an uplifting and loving welcome, and I took it very personally.

What was more beautiful, however, was a small shrine to Mother Mary tucked away in a small chapel in a back corner of the church. In the chapel was a tender yet powerful statue of Mary that moved me to tears with its loving emanations. Every time I visited, I made a point of praying there.

While sitting there I was reassured that I was on my path and what was happening now was in divine alignment with my soul. I hadn't made a mistake—the divorce wasn't a failure, just a destined ending, and it was simply time for my journey to continue in a different direction. I felt that God had better plans for me than I had for myself and was glad for it. Each time I came and prayed there I was guided to keep releasing the past, keep loving myself, keep accepting and forgiving the painful experiences in my heart and the judgments that went along with them (mostly toward myself), and keep trusting that in the end all would be well for all of us. These quiet conversations between Mother Mary and me were deeply reassuring, and I agreed to listen, as difficult as it was at times. I knew I was being given a blessing with this guidance and simply needed to hold tight to it as I continued to fumble through each day, adjusting to new circumstances, learning a new culture, and freeing up a new me.

Time to Commit

Before we knew it, it was the middle of March and we were in the final three weeks of our Airbnb stay in the Old Lady. It was time to decide if we wanted to make a bigger commitment and move to Paris for good or go back to Chicago and resume life there. Paris won out hands down. Neither of us had anything to go back to, save for my other daughter, Sonia, and she promised to visit us every other month at least and had already done so once. So we were free to settle in and not look back.

As much as it was so annoying to live there in so many ways, I first asked the Airbnb host if we could rent the Old Lady on a proper lease, which we needed in order to get our long-stay visa. I was used to her by now, as well as the neighborhood, and was reluctant to up and move. In asking, I realized what a creature of habit I was underneath it all and how I clung to things, even if they were not the best for me. I needed to learn to let go.

As it turned out, I had a chance to learn that lesson—it was *not* possible to stay, as the owner had rented the Old Lady for most of the year ahead. I accepted that it was once again time for change and set about finding a new place to rent before we went back to Chicago to retrieve the rest of our belongings.

With the help of a few local real estate agencies, we began our search for a furnished apartment we could rent outright. As with the Old Lady, every apartment was described as a veritable oasis of French class and sophistication, but upon seeing the apartments within our price range, we were more often than not completely grossed out. With each disappointment, the rent I was willing to pay crept up, as I figured it would be worth it to let other things go, like regular shopping in pharmacies and daily pastries and chocolates, if the apartment was nice enough.

Since we were not committed to staying in the 18th, all of Paris was open to us as we searched. We looked at apartments in the Marais (too noisy); in the 17th (too remote and not that interesting); in the 9th, where we really wanted to live (too small and really run down); and beyond. Spreading our wings, we ended up visiting an apartment in the 7th, along avenue Bourdonnais near the École Militaire, a bourgeois area we had never traveled to, even on our nightly walks, and knew nothing about.

"This feels very far away," Sabrina said with an air of suspicion as we traveled across the Seine from the right bank to the left. As our taxi whizzed by, we caught a glimpse of the statue of Princess Diana near the place de l'Alma, where she died in a car accident all those years ago.

"I agree," I said. "But we might as well just go and see it. We are almost there as it is, and we have to find a place soon because we are running out of time. This is the only one left on our list for the day, and I have no other apartments lined up to see."

Five minutes later, the taxi dropped us off on the corner of avenue Bourdonnais and rue de Grenelle, and the driver pointed to a building on our left and across the street, behind a beautiful wrought-iron gate. There, waiting to meet us, was our agent, a young American woman living in Paris.

Sabrina was reluctant as we stepped out of the taxi, but I was optimistic. "Hello," Emily said, greeting us warmly, unlike the more reserved French realtors we had met with before. It was refreshing to hear a familiar language and feel a familiar warmth as we were shown in.

The lobby of the apartment building was small but elegant. Immediately to the left was the *gardien*'s apartment, and to the right the entire wall was covered in gilded mirror, with a row of fresh plants and flowers along the bottom, a marble floor beneath our feet.

We then approached a second set of doors, which Emily opened with another key. Once past that door we saw a teeny, tiny elevator directly ahead and, to the left, a narrow curved staircase leading up, much like in our current building.

Emily asked if we wanted to ride in the elevator, as the apartment was on the fifth floor, but we declined as it seemed much too small for all three of us to get into. We said we would walk and meet her up there. Then we began the winding journey upward.

While we were very used to walking, by the time we reached the fifth floor, we were out of breath. The elevator doors opened just as we arrived, and we all converged in front of the apartment door at the same time.

There were two apartments on each floor, and Emily explained that the other apartment belonged to the building owner. We would be neighbors if we took this apartment.

Sabrina and I raised our eyebrows at each other when we heard this, knowing how at times, given our Latin tempers, we were prone to explosive, albeit short, exchanges, which no doubt would be heard by him if we weren't careful.

The apartment took our breath away. With brilliant sunlight streaming in, it felt brand-new, and that alone was refreshing beyond belief. Many of the apartments we had seen reeked of mold; had broken lights, dirty carpets, and ratty furniture; and were in deplorable condition overall. By comparison, the Old Lady looked as luxurious as she had been advertised to be. But this was another world altogether.

For one thing, the ceilings were 14 feet high, which felt so elegant and French. There was a large entryway and, to the left, a curious photo of a woman strolling down a mountain path, her back to us, wearing a sort of lederhosen-type top, hair in braids, and naked from the butt down atop some extremely high-heeled shoes. She was swinging a purse alongside as if it were an everyday thing to go out like this.

Then in front of us and slightly to the right was a large buffet. On either side of the buffet were two sets of double doors, both leading into a double salon. There was a beautifully but simply furnished living room in the front salon, with two long, chocolate-brown velvet couches face-to-face, a coffee table, and a large wall-mounted TV above the fireplace. In the back half of the double salon was a large dining-room table, a small chair in the corner, another fireplace on the back wall, and a set of French doors that opened up to a small balcony.

Next we were led to three separate and very *large* bedrooms. Two were on the left side of the apartment and each had its own set of floor-to-ceiling doors leading to a little balcony. The bedrooms were furnished simply with a queen bed, an IKEA desk and dresser, and a wardrobe for clothes.

In the back was the third bedroom, with its own set of nearly floor-to-ceiling French windows, which looked out on a back courtyard. It connected to one of the front bedrooms through a bathroom.

Continuing the tour, we were next shown another separate toilet, painted curiously enough in bright red, and a second full bath with both a shower (placed up high) and a deep tub, all absolutely brand spanking new.

Finally, leading us back toward the front near the entryway, Emily showed us a very large kitchen with all new appliances, a washer *and* dryer, a spacious countertop, and many cabinets filled with pots, pans, and anything else a gourmet cook might need. On the back wall was a large window overlooking the back courtyard, and a back door.

It was spectacular, and very, very, *very* expensive.

Emily decided to give us a moment to discuss things and stepped away. Sabrina was cautious. "Mom, it's so expensive and we don't know this area. It seems a little sedate. Are you sure you want to take this on? Are we sure we even like this neighborhood? We don't know anything about it."

We whisper-discussed the apartment for a few more minutes, then Emily stepped back into the room and said, "It's quite a beautiful place. I have never seen a furnished apartment as nice as this one for rent." I knew she was telling the truth. We had seen quite a few ourselves, and this was far better than any of the others by a long stretch.

Loving it but knowing I simply could not afford it, I turned to Emily and spontaneously said, "Please tell the landlord that we are wonderful tenants whom he will like very much, and then ask him if he can significantly lower the rent. After all, we will be long-term and not short-term renters, as most furnished apartment renters are, and that might appeal to him. He will probably like that."

Emily was shocked by my request. "Oh, I don't think he will do that," she said. "It just isn't done."

"Well, just please ask him," I insisted. "All he can say is no, and if that's his answer, we won't be able to afford it anyway. We have nothing to lose."

Emily agreed that she would ask but was not at all encouraging. If anything, she was quite the opposite. "Shall I keep you in mind if other furnished apartments come up?" she asked as we stepped outside and she closed up the apartment.

"Just focus on this for now," I answered, then turned and ran down the stairs, as we had to quickly jump in a taxi and head back to the 18th to begin work.

In the taxi, we turned to each another and said, "Oh my God. What a beautiful apartment!" bubbling over with excitement over the possibility it could become ours.

Knowing full well how I tend to jump into things before thinking them through, Sabrina said, "It is a beautiful apartment, Mom, but are you sure we can afford it?"

"We can if he cuts the rent as we asked him to," I answered. "Let's light a candle and pray. If it is meant to be ours, it'll happen, and we will know soon enough one way or another."

We received no response from Emily for the next two days, despite my sending her annoying e-mails asking over and over again if she had an answer for us.

Finally, on the third day, I got a call from Emily saying that, to her surprise, the landlord had agreed to our terms after all. We couldn't believe it. She couldn't either. We were definitely moving on up, and I was thrilled beyond belief. "Thank you, angels!" Sabrina and I both screamed out at the same time, then high-fived one another. We had a brand-new place to live, and it was everything I had dreamed of when deciding to live in Paris. It was not that much more expensive than the Old Lady and was clearly a sign that we were supposed to be here and were being helped by our angels every step of the way.

We went to Emily's office the next day and signed all the papers before work. We had a mountain of stuff to send the landlord before the lease would be executed, but we were assured that as soon as the papers were received and our security deposit cleared, they would e-mail the lease and we would be free to get our long-stay visas.

Emily was so happy to have sealed the deal that she agreed when we asked if we could leave some of our bags in her office while we returned to Chicago to get the rest of our stuff. She even offered to make sure they would be waiting for us at the new apartment when we returned, which was another hassle taken off our plate.

Preparing to leave the Old Lady was a little bittersweet. She had been such a comfort as we ran from our misery and straight into her arms three months earlier.

We had come to love our neighborhood and feel at home here, so leaving it felt a little sad. We would absolutely return, we told ourselves as we packed up our belongings, and we meant it.

The fire drill part of living in Paris was coming to a close. We would soon be on our way back to Chicago to get the rest of our stuff ready to bring back in a month, after getting our visas. I was also going to put the house up for sale and shut the door on my old life once and for all.

Part Three

THE OLD MAN

Cutting the Cords

Returning to Chicago felt like going back to a haunted house. We had 30 days to clear out, put the Victorian on the market, pack the rest of our stuff to bring back with us, and obtain our long-term visas, all while working with clients every day. It was a daunting whirlwind of a challenge, but I was determined to get through it as I now had a new life beckoning.

Now that I really was moving to Paris, I was ready to let go of everything. What I didn't realize was the amount of junk that a three-story house can accumulate over the years. There were closets and closets full of seemingly endless stuff. Having lived in the Old Lady for the past three months, I realized just how little I needed to be comfortable. The less stuff I had, the more freedom came with it. And freedom is what I craved now more than anything.

I had beds and furniture and paintings and tables and closets full of clothes and books and lamps and pots and pans and dishes and baskets and baskets and baskets (don't ask me why)— and these were only the things *inside* the house. The garage was full, as well.

After giving away what I could to friends, I hired several guys to come and clear out the rest. They knew families in need, so were happy to take away as much as they could. I could feel the layers of the past being peeled off with each load out the door. Room by room, floor by floor, the closets and drawers were emptied, the furniture was moved out, and my life opened up. It was physically and emotionally painful and exhausting, but I was grateful for the chance to so thoroughly learn to let go of my earthly attachments and trust all would be well.

In the end Sabrina and I pared down to four large suitcases each of stuff to bring with us. We decided that this wasn't too bad, given that we had both just given away our entire previous lives. Our American tendency to want and have way more than we need was falling to the wayside. Our new life would be simple and unencumbered. We called ourselves "Free Birds" and made the song our anthem.

Our next task was obtaining our long-stay visas. It just required a lot of paperwork proving that we would not be bums and could afford to be there. It was a bit of a hassle, but soon enough I had it all in order to submit to the French consulate along with our passports; our visas would be mailed back to us. If we were lucky, they would take about two weeks to process, a delay I hadn't expected. We turned the paperwork in exactly 14 days before our departure date. Handing everything over, we held our breath and hoped it would be returned in time.

Our flight was on Saturday and it was the Thursday before and still we had not received our passports with visas in the mail. On Friday, as the last boxes were being carried out the door and sent to the Salvation Army, the mail arrived and in it were our passports. It was perfect timing and seemed like a sign. Out with the old and in with the new.

The next morning, with a For Sale sign on the front lawn of the house, we set off once again back to Paris, this time for an entire year at least.

We arrived at the airport with our eight big suitcases and checked in for our flight. Once we had our boarding passes in hand, we texted Julien the driver and let him know that once again we were on our way back and in need of his services, only this time we would need *two* vans to carry our stuff to the new apartment. Two minutes later he texted back, "Hello, Mesdames *Americaines*. I will be there with pleasure." Then he said he would come with a second van and meet us in the same place as he had before.

With that settled, for the first time in a month I relaxed. I was really excited, a little incredulous, a little apprehensive, and completely committed to creating a brand-new life in an entirely new part of Paris. It was all a little surreal, yet I felt fully alive and ready for the adventure, whatever may come.

As we lifted off I was amazed at just how powerful it is to have something totally new, uncharted, and exciting to look forward to when your life falls apart. Our new apartment, with its tall ceilings, newly painted white walls, French doors with balconies across the entire length of the apartment, three large bedrooms *with* heat, brand-new furniture, a washer *and* dryer, and yes, even the photo of the naked-butt girl in the lederhosen all promised something new and better. Even the weird huge paintings of eyeballs staring at us that hung in all the bedrooms, painted by the landlord's wife, beckoned me forward, whispering, "The best is yet to come, Sonia, so don't look back."

More than just the beautiful apartment, I looked forward to the blank slate on which to create a brand-new life this beautiful new apartment offered me. I had no idea what the new neighborhood would be like, or if we would even fit in there, but that didn't matter. No matter what was in store, our new calm, grounded apartment settled my anxiety and soothed my emotions. Like an oasis in the desert of my pain, it beckoned me forward with its hint at the possibility of finding a more beautiful future in store. Following that promise was exactly what I needed right now. It gave me faith and encouragement and helped me believe my heart would eventually heal.

Rue Belgrade

As soon as Sabrina and I exited baggage claim with our mountain of luggage, we were met with Julien's smiling face. He took one look at us and the two porters behind us, pushing our excess luggage along, and said, "Oh wow! You weren't kidding, we need two vans."

Grabbing the cart that I was pushing and signaling to his partner, Hugo, to grab Sabrina's cart from her, he waved his arm to the porters to follow him, and our wagon train rolled out the door and toward the two vans waiting just outside.

It took a bit of work and creativity, but soon all the bags were stuffed into one or the other van, and we were on our way. Julien was delighted that we had moved from the 18th, and wasted no time in telling us that we had really, *really* moved up since our last apartment. In fact, he said, our new apartment was in a real snob *quartier*. Everyone who lived there, according to him, was very conservative, old school, and a bit cold and boring.

Sabrina and I looked apprehensively at each other as he rambled on. We were a lot of things, but cold, old school, and boring were not among them. "Oh well." We shrugged. If we didn't like the *quartier*, we would just walk to another one. Paris wasn't that big, and no *quartier* would dampen our mood. After all, it was *Paris*. And besides, we were way too far in to second-guess ourselves now.

Still, after all the excitement of the last *quartier*, we hoped we hadn't made a huge mistake.

We didn't have much time to worry about it before we found ourselves standing in front of our new building.

With the door code e-mailed to us by the new landlord in hand, we let ourselves in and then rang the inside doorbell to let him know we had just arrived. In the meantime, Julien and Hugo unloaded the bags from the car and piled them up behind us in the *rez de chaussée.*

In two minutes, the landlord exited the tiny elevator and said, "Hello. I'm Jean Luc, your new landlord. You must be Sonia and Sabrina." He was an unusually tall, handsome man around 50, with a full head of hair, a big smile, and a warm, easygoing manner, who spoke perfect English with a wonderful French accent. "Welcome to your new home." He then glanced at Julien and Hugo and said, "You guys can take these bags to the service elevator in the back and send them up, and we will meet you upstairs." He then took them down a small hall next to where we were standing and reappeared 10 seconds later.

"Alrighty then," he said, "that's settled." Then, turning back to us, he said, *"On y va."* The next thing we knew, all three of us were stuffed as tight as sardines in a tin can in the teeny-weeny elevator. We were so close to one another that our faces nearly touched and we didn't dare open our mouths for fear our airplane breath would blow Jean Luc away. We just cast our eyes downward and said nothing while he cast his upward, equally silent, as we *slowly* climbed to the fifth floor.

Once the external doors opened, we exploded out of the elevator, all three of us exhaling simultaneously. "Here we are," Jean Luc said cheerfully as he took the apartment keys from his pocket. "Home sweet home, as they say in the U.S." He swept us in with a grand gesture and then walked us into the kitchen and opened the back door, where we found Julien waiting on the smallest landing atop a shaky-looking winding staircase, with a few bags stacked in front of him. The service elevator was already finding its way back to the first floor for the next round.

We could hardly believe we were here. The apartment was nicer than we had remembered. And so big! It was also so much brighter and sunnier than when we saw it a month earlier, when it was still dark and gloomy outside. And in the living room were our bags sent over by Emily.

After we took off our coats, Jean Luc showed us how to use the TV, the oven, the microwave, the Internet (which thankfully worked well in all the rooms in the apartment), and the washer *and* dryer, all of which were brand-new. It felt positively decadent to be here after our time spent in the Old Lady.

As he showed us around, he told us this building was built by his grandfather in the middle 1800s and had been in his family ever since. He went on to explain that he had just renovated this apartment and we were its first tenants. It felt so good to enter a place with no one else's energy in it. It was the perfect place to start anew.

Our heads were spinning by the time the final bags were carried in. We sent Julien and Hugo on their way with a good old American hug, raising Jean Luc's eyebrow. He then assessed the mountain before us and said, "I hope you can find space for everything in here."

"I'm sure we will," I assured him, wondering the same thing myself, as I could tell from looking around there was nowhere near the closet space we were used to having at home. There were, however, two rows of shallow floor-to-ceiling built-in closets along the walls leading to the back bedrooms. In Sabrina's bedroom-to-be, there was also a large armoire, but no closet in the third bedroom. We would just have to make do. Fortunately, we knew how, as we had already been trained at the Old Lady.

I asked if there was a storage space for the luggage, once it was emptied, as eight large suitcases took up a lot of room. "Of course," he said, "we will make room in the *cave.*"

The next thing we knew, we were all stuffed *back* into the world's smallest elevator and on our way down. Once on the ground floor, we were led to another back stairway leading farther down and into a mud-walled, very moldy, very stinky, ancient-feeling basement with a few ramshackle doors with cheap locks on them. He opened one of the doors and shoved aside some large boxes and things, then said, "Yes. This should do. You can put your luggage in here. Just call me when you are ready, and I'll bring you back down."

When we got back upstairs, we didn't have the energy to do anything but plop down on each of the two very large, very comfortable, very new brown velour sofas facing each other and stare, first at each other, then around the place, then at each other again, speechless the entire time.

Finally, I blurted out, "I think we'll like it here. Everything is so perfect."

Sabrina agreed. "It's great, Mom. I love it already."

Just then the doorbell rang, and it was Jean Luc again. He popped his head in. "Hello, ladies. Want to go to lunch? My treat."

We burst out laughing, surprised and delighted that he had asked. Starving by now, we readily agreed. The next minute, we had our coats on and were once again stuffed *back* into the mini elevator, heading down. By this last elevator ride we felt we were best friends with Jean Luc and said so the minute the doors opened. We all laughed, as we were all thinking the same thing as we headed out the door and directly across the street to a small Italian restaurant called Gusto's.

"We eat here all the time," Jean Luc said as we walked in. The minute the waitress saw Jean Luc, she walked over to him and gave him two kisses, one on each cheek, in a typical French-style welcome. He turned to us and said, "Regina, this is Sonia and Sabrina, my new tenants. I'm sure you will see them here often." Regina was a young, serious-looking woman with such extremely droopy eyelids that she looked as though she had just woken up. She blinked slowly as she said, *"Bonjour,"* and then gave us kisses on each cheek as well, which really surprised us. Two minutes later the restaurant owner emerged from the back room and came over to say hello to Jean Luc. He was clearly Regina's father, as he looked even sleepier than Regina did. Again we were introduced, but the father, while gracious, was more conservative, so no kisses were forthcoming. Instead he sent over glasses of red wine to welcome us.

We were so delighted to be welcomed so warmly, we could hardly believe our good fortune, as this was not typically the French way. It took almost three months to know anyone by name in the 18th and no one had ever invited us anywhere. Now, only 30 minutes after we had arrived, we were being taken out to lunch and making friends. This was extraordinarily unusual and wasn't lost on us.

We ordered pizzas, salads, and more red wine, and settled in to learn more about Jean Luc and his family as we ate. In his unusually easygoing manner, he told us his wife's name was Alice and that they had a 12-year-old daughter named Alex, who was presently in Saint Louis, Missouri, for two weeks on a school exchange program. He laughed and told us that they were not particularly religious, and the family she was staying with was very Catholic.

He said she had called and told Jean Luc and Alice that, as her host family was getting ready for Sunday Mass, she asked to stay home. She told the family, *"Ce n'est pas mon style,"* meaning, "It's not my style," when asked why she didn't want to go with them. I laughed out loud. It was so *French*.

Jean Luc told us he had formerly been an engineer but recently quit his job when he inherited both this building and one other, and was now a full-time landlord and renovator. He was so genuinely open and friendly. Over lunch he offered to help us get French cell phones set up and open a local bank account in the neighborhood, all of which we now needed to do. I told him I was truly grateful and warned him that helping to get us settled might be a lot more work than he bargained for. "No problem," he assured me. "I want my tenants to be happy."

So much for all those projections about stuffy French people in the 7th. Jean Luc was open and generous, which also let me know that our own energy was improving or this wouldn't be happening, as the outside always reflects the inside. That was the most encouraging of all.

After pizza and wine, both Sabrina and I started fading fast. Luckily we had only to walk across the street to be home to take a nap, one more big plus for this apartment. We felt happy and relieved to begin this next leg of our adventure so warmly welcomed and well fed. When we reentered the building, we now happily stuffed ourselves into the elevator with Jean Luc, too tired to walk up five floors, or care. We had bonded in that elevator, after all, and by now we all had garlic breath.

Back in the apartment, as we started to slowly unpack a few things from our bags, all I could say was, "Thank you, angels." This was clearly meant to be.

Exhausted, we stopped unpacking after only a few minutes and promptly found our way to our *respective* large, *warm* bedrooms, yelling across the hall to each other to have a nice nap. After all the turmoil we had faced over the past several months, it felt good to be in such a solid place, with its six-inch-thick stone walls; its heavy front door; its glistening, winding staircase; its large French windows; its quiet comfort and reassurance; and its super friendly and welcoming landlord/friend just across the hall in case we needed anything. It was all so very new, but it signaled to me that I was absolutely on the right path and had made the right decision to move here at this point in my life, even if I hadn't planned on it. It felt as though God had plans for me, and they were far better than my own. It was a leap of faith to be sure, but I was really glad I took it.

Rue Cler

Waking up after a few hours' nap, we decided it was time to explore the neighborhood and get some groceries and household supplies for the apartment so we could settle in before the shops closed at 7 P.M.

Before we left, we stepped outside onto the tiny balcony off the living room to check the weather and look around. Below us was avenue Bourdonnais, lined with big, bright, freshly budding trees. To our left a few blocks away was the Seine River, and to our right at an equal distance was the École Militaire, a vast complex of buildings housing military training facilities, built by Louis XV and still in use.

Though we couldn't see it from our vantage point, starting at the École Militaire and running all the way to the Eiffel Tower was the Champ-de-Mars, one of the most beautiful and iconic places in all of Paris, and the place where Parisians—along with hundreds of thousands of tourists—gathered to relax and play, picnic, watch sporting events on a huge outdoor screen, and enjoy Bastille Day fireworks year after year. It was hard to believe that this was now our *backyard!*

We threw our jackets back on, as in spite of it being spring, it was still quite cool outside, and headed out the door once again, this time taking the winding stairs down instead of the elevator. As we descended we took in the elegant craftsmanship of the building, feeling as though Jean Luc's grandfather's prideful presence walked with us, pointing out all the fine details.

Each floor had two apartments just like ours, with huge, dark oak double doors with bronze hardware polished to a brilliant shine leading into each one. The floors were highly polished oak as well, with a deep red carpet runner down the middle of the stairs and on each landing all the way to the first floor (thank God, as I didn't want to go luging headfirst down another round of steps if I could help it). The teeny elevator went from the first floor to the floor above us, with the stairs leading up to a seventh. On the top floor was a lone apartment where Jean Luc told us his mother lived. On the far wall of the stairwell, from the top floor all the way to the *rez de chaussée,* was a beautiful stained-glass window.

As we gleefully hopped down the stairs, taking it all in, we suddenly realized how loud we were being. We were so enthusiastic that we were nearly screaming at each other with excitement and had to force ourselves to quiet down lest we upset the neighbors and get off on the wrong foot with them. After all, even though Jean Luc may have been warm and welcoming, the building really did feel quite reserved, and our boisterous energy felt completely out of place. If we weren't careful, we might come across to our neighbors as the loud Americans that we were.

Once we got to the main floor, we met up with a woman who appeared to be the *gardien* of the building. We introduced ourselves to her as the new tenants on the fifth floor, and she politely said, *"Bonjour, Mesdames,"* but didn't smile and showed little desire to speak to us beyond that. She was a very elegant older woman wearing a beautiful gray cashmere sweater and a scarf around her neck atop a dark skirt and sensible heels. Her perfectly coiffed hair looked as if she had just come from the salon. Glancing at our gym shoes and jeans, you could tell from her ever-so-slight sneer that she didn't think much of how we dressed. In all fairness, we did look a mess. For a split second I wished I had on my white button-down shirt at least. Too bad I gave it away to the woman who ran the laundromat where we washed our sheets before we moved out of the Old Lady.

Oh, well, we are who we are, I thought as we headed out the door. Once outside we glanced around, since we had no idea where we were. We had never been to this part of Paris, so it seemed as though we were in a brand-new city, an altogether different Paris than that of the earlier three months. Excited to discover our new neighborhood, we crossed avenue Bourdonnais and started down rue de Grenelle toward rue Cler, the great market street we were told about when we rented the apartment in March and had yet to discover.

Walking along, we noticed both sides of rue de Grenelle were filled with beautiful shops and food markets. In the space of two blocks there was a greengrocer, a *boulangerie,* a butcher, a small convenience shop, a cheese shop, a wine shop, several Italian markets with fresh homemade Italian food ready to take out, several Italian restaurants, two beautiful flower shops, as well as a great French pharmacy at the end of the street, on the corner of avenue Bosquet.

Boy, the French really know how to live in style, I thought, feeling like a kid in a candy store, relishing all the fabulous foods I would be enjoying in no time.

Like beautiful flowers, beautiful food was another *essential* here. A delicious meal was the heart of French life. I even read once that French people spend an average of seven hours a week eating meals together, while Americans spend an average of two. There was nothing "fast" about food here. It was another basic of life that people savored.

It felt as if we'd hit the fresh food lottery as we strolled along rue de Grenelle. It got even better once we crossed avenue Bosquet and finally discovered rue Cler.

We immediately felt as though we had walked into an old-world village and original market smack in the middle of Paris. Under our feet were the original cobblestones leading into a pedestrian area about four city blocks long, filled with a wonderful selection of even more specialty food shops: greengrocers, fishmongers, butchers, cheese shops, wine shops, flower shops, chocolate shops, and more. There was even a shop devoted exclusively to the sale of whipped cream, and it was very busy at the moment.

The street was packed with shoppers strolling along with their *petits* chariots, as if led by their noses, sniffing the fresh fruits and vegetables, the cheeses, the fresh fish, even the baguettes hot out of the oven, like bloodhounds on the hunt.

Sprinkled in between these marvelous food markets and shops were many quintessential French cafés with large terraces in front, all packed to the brim with cigarette-smoking locals, students, and tourists, the latter evidenced by their cameras and selfie sticks. People were sipping coffee or glasses of wine while watching the parade of shoppers, tourists, and children whiz by, many on little scooters, their parents following right behind them on big scooters of their own.

We were immediately charmed by the atmosphere and knew we would find ourselves right at home here in no time. As for shopping, there were so many options to choose from and the food looked so fresh and gorgeous, our brains could hardly take it all in.

This *quartier* embodied the quintessentially classic, yet earthy, old-school Paris captured in vintage postcards sent around the world. Life here was beautiful, sophisticated, reserved, and elegant, but not so much that it wasn't inviting. Unlike the chaos and color of the 18th, the 7th had an entirely different, almost uptight Parisian vibe. One in which people wore a lot of beige, spoke quietly, and avoided eye contact on the street. It was fascinating, seductive, and felt very exclusive, hinting at all sorts of delicious and indulgent treats if we behaved ourselves.

Fascinated by all that we were discovering, we ventured farther in spite of our jet lag. Within minutes we found ourselves strolling down rue Dominique, which was lined with chic independent clothing and shoe boutiques; beautiful *libraries* selling exquisite wrapping papers, fountain pens, coffee-table books and journals; and one great neighborhood restaurant or café after another.

Feeling as though we were on a treasure hunt, we followed the beckoning sights and smells down adjacent streets and soon found ourselves surrounded by art galleries, antique shops, and designer furniture stores catering to the obviously *very* rich and famous.

We emerged from the narrow streets to a grand plaza in which sat the vast military structure called Les Invalides, originally a hospital and home for retired French soldiers, and more famously the place where Napoleon Bonaparte is buried. Directly in front of Les Invalides was Pont Alexander III, the most ornate bridge in all of Paris, connecting the Champs-Elysées to the 7th *quartier*, where we were now standing. It took our breath away, it was so insanely beautiful.

Five minutes later we found ourselves at the beginning of the boulevard St Germaine, considered the heart of the chic 7th *quartier*, and strolled past both Les Deux Magots and Café de Flore, cafés made famous by their regulars, Jean Paul Sartre, Ernest Hemingway, Pablo Picasso, and Simone de Beauvoir among other well-known artists and writers. As a writer I imagined myself sitting among them.

This was such a far cry from where we had just come from that it felt as if we were in another movie altogether. Exciting, intense, inviting, and intimidating all at once, the 7th captivated all our senses until we felt positively drunk on the relentless aesthetic stimulation.

Eventually we tired from so much walking after such a long flight, so we wound our way back. As we turned back toward our apartment, we decided to pick up a few items on rue Cler to help us settle in before we ran out of energy.

Not sure where to begin once we arrived, the first thing we did was stop at a small shop called Cler Affaire, halfway down rue Cler, which carried all sorts of household items. We bought a new chariot for carrying our soon-to-be-purchased groceries home, as we had left the last one with the Old Lady.

Strolling along with chariot #2, we began studying the individual shops along both sides of the street, taking them in one at a time, slowly getting the feel and the mood of this marvelous little village.

It was very different from rue des Martyrs—less chaotic, more subdued, and, yes, more bourgeois. In other words, more uptight and conservative.

Having walked from one end to the other and back, which was about the equivalent of about four city blocks in the U.S., and feeling we'd had enough for the day, we settled on making a simple dinner. We bought a few vine-fresh tomatoes, some fresh French green beans, and mixed lettuce at the organic greengrocer on the corner of Cler and Grenelle. Then we stopped for a wheel of fresh creamy brie from the *fromagerie,* or cheese shop, on the other side of Cler and a piping-hot, golden roasted chicken right off the spit from the *boucherie,* or butcher shop, on rue de Grenelle as we walked back toward our apartment.

Of course, no meal would be complete without a fresh-from-the-oven baguette and a good bottle of Bordeaux wine, so we stopped at a wine shop called Nicolas on the corner of Grenelle and then, without missing a beat, crossed to the other side for a baguette and macarons from the *boulangerie* next door.

With chariot loaded up with "goodies" and pinching ourselves that this was our new neighborhood, we nearly sang our way back to the apartment. Living here would be so much easier than living in the 18th, and after the stressful events of the recent months, all I wanted now was to have my days unfold in the easiest way possible.

Granted, moving to a new country, especially France, was probably not the *easiest* of choices. But it *was* the easiest path to forgetting the past and being totally immersed in the beautiful present, and that was healing in and of itself.

Salut, Grand-père

Back at the apartment we made a quick dinner and tried to unpack our bags and settle in a little more. We fought for the closets and settled into the ones we each won, stuffing them with our clothes and shoes.

This was home now, and we were still trying to get our heads around it. We turned on some music as we unpacked and more than once asked each other if we knew what the heck we were doing as we shook our heads in disbelief that we had actually fully *moved* here.

By 10 P.M. we were totally spent. It was time to go to bed. Retiring to our respective bedrooms, we yelled good night to each other and shut off the lights.

Five minutes later, the hall light between our bedrooms turned back on.

"Sabrina, is that you?" I asked, annoyed by the bright light streaming into my room just as I was falling asleep.

"No, I thought it was you," she replied.

"That's weird," I said as I got up and turned the light back off.

Just as I lay back down and barely closed my eyes, the hall light turned on once again.

"Mom, is that you?" Sabrina called out.

"No, Sabrina. I just shut off the light," I replied.

Now both of us got out of bed and walked to the hallway between our rooms, wondering what was going on. We turned the lights on and off a few times, making sure we knew how to work them, wondering if perhaps we hadn't fully turned the lights off in the first place. Certain that this was not the case, I shut off the light once again and we both turned to go back to bed. Five seconds later, before we even got in bed—snap—the lights came back on. We both spun around and met in the hallway once again, eyes wide as saucers as we looked at one another, agog at what had just happened. Given that there was no timer attached to these ancient overhead lights, it made no sense that they would just pop on. We felt a spirit in the air, and our eyes widened even more. "It's Jean Luc's grandfather—*Grand-père!*" we exclaimed at the same time.

"He wants us to know he's here," Sabrina said, and the light got brighter.

"I think you're right," I answered. "I wonder if he's just saying hello." The question was directed more to him than to Sabrina.

The lights flickered.

"Okay, Grand-père, enough. We're happy you are here, but we need to go to sleep now," I said. Sabrina was laughing so hard she couldn't speak. "We are happy to be here, by the way. Oh, and thank you for such a warm welcome."

Once again I shut off the light, and we went to bed.

Ten seconds later Sabrina called out nervously, "Mom, can I sleep in your room tonight?"

"Of course," I said, laughing. "Hurry up. I'm so tired."

She grabbed her pillow and ran across the hall. We both lay quietly in bed, in the dark, half waiting for the light to pop back on.

Fifteen minutes passed and it was still dark.

Finally relaxing, I decided Grand-père had gone to bed as well. Just then, the light popped back on again.

"Aw, Grand-père, give me a break," I said out loud as I got out of bed for the third time and shut off the light once again. "I need to go to sleep now." No sooner had I turned back to bed, when once more the light popped back on. "Good night, Grand-père," I said firmly as I shut my door, leaving the light on. "I'm too tired to play with you tonight."

The light was still on as I fell asleep.

In the morning when I woke up, the light was off.

"Apparently Grand-père was having fun last night," I announced to Sabrina. "Seems he is sleeping now."

I turned the light on and then off. I waited for him to turn it back on, but nothing happened. It stayed off all day long and I no longer felt Grand-père's presence. I wondered if he would visit again, or if he was just the welcoming committee.

He visited again the very next night. Ten minutes after we shut off the hall light for bed, it popped back on. Just as it had the night before, the game went on for a few minutes, with us shutting off the light and him turning it back on, until we surrendered and said, "Good night, Grand-père. We are going to sleep," and then shut our doors and left the light on.

It was always off in the morning. It happened every few nights or so, and soon became another comforting aspect of our new home. And so we began a new adventure in our new apartment, which we lovingly named "the Old Man."

It's Official

One of our first objectives once we settled into the Old Man was to scope out the area and find our new local café. Everyone in Paris has a preferred café or two, and just as we'd had KB Café in the 18th, we now needed to locate one in our new neighborhood.

The obvious place to look, of course, was on rue Cler, so each day we tried one of the cafés along the street. We started with the classic Café Central located halfway down rue Cler, between rue de Grenelle where it began and avenue de la Motte-Picquet, where rue Cler ended. Café Central was the most beautiful café, with a wide wraparound terrace perfect for watching people in all directions, but it had terrible coffee, so we reluctantly ruled it out. We then moved on to Café du Marché just next door, much smaller but also with an impressive terrace on which to sit and watch people go by, but the service was terrible and we were not in the mood to start the day at yet another rude café, so that, too, was soon out. Finally, we tried Le Petit Cler, a small, charming café with a little terrace right across from our favorite organic fruit and vegetable market just off rue de Grenelle. To our delight, they served wonderful, large steaming cups of café au lait and delicious omelets, and the atmosphere was delightful. We were sold. This was definitely going to be our new café. We went there every morning for the next three mornings. On Sunday, however, a week after we had arrived, we showed up as usual only to be met at the door by the café manager, a very tall, serious-looking bald man who watched over the café like a guard dog. He sternly asked us if we had a reservation.

Of course we didn't have a reservation, and who ever did at a café? (We learned later that people do. Lots of them.) When we replied no, he said in a very arrogant, harsh voice that it was Mother's Day and there was simply no place for us.

I don't know if it was not being allowed in or his dismissive tone and behavior toward us or the fact that I was still feeling jet-lagged and overwhelmed, and underneath it all sensitive to any rejection, but his abrupt dismissal felt like a slap in the face. It took me by such surprise and offended me so much that I said so.

"You are mean, *Monsieur*," I blurted out in French. "I'm a mother, too."

My comment took him equally by surprise and stopped him in his tracks. He obviously had a certain image of himself, and "mean" wasn't part of it.

"I'm not mean, *Madame*," he replied defensively, suddenly aware of how he came across.

"*Mais oui*, you are," I repeated, feeling both very immature and very American.

"*Mais non, pas du tout*," he insisted, once again.

"Then please don't speak so harshly to us," I answered in French. "*Ce n'est pas gentil*."

We were like two five-year-olds accusing each other of not being nice.

Now needing to prove to us that he *wasn't* mean, he suddenly changed his mind about the availability of a table and escorted us to a small one outside. We sat down and composed ourselves. I felt embarrassed at my outburst and turned to Sabrina and said, "Great, this is my favorite café and now we can't come here ever again."

Sabrina wouldn't hear of it. "Nonsense, Mom. He was not '*gentil*,' and he didn't have to speak to us that way. We can come back any time we want."

I wasn't so sure as I sat and sipped my delicious, hot, steaming café au lait. I certainly would have to apologize for my outburst in order to show up again. But the café au lait was so good, I decided that I would.

It took a few days, but I summoned the courage to return. Sabrina had left town to visit a friend in Australia, and I found myself alone in Paris for the first time since we arrived. I woke up, got dressed quickly, and headed back to Cler for my morning café au lait, hoping the manager wouldn't be there.

He was the first person to greet me (of course) and sat me down with an awkward and cool, but polite, *"Bonjour, Madame,"* followed by my equally awkward and cooler, equally polite, *"Bonjour, Monsieur."* At least *that* was over.

I sat quietly and sipped my café au lait and enjoyed some eggs for breakfast, watching the world on rue Cler go by. It was a new-found luxury to start my day out so leisurely and certainly something I never did in America. It was positively healthy to live at this much slower pace, and I found it to be just what I needed to ground and align me with who I was discovering I wanted to be today. After an hour, and a second large café au lait, it was time to pay and go.

I reached for my purse only to discover, to my horror, that in my hurry I had left my wallet at home. *Oh no,* I thought, panicking. *First I accuse the manager of being mean, and now I don't have any money to pay my bill.* This was the worst thing that could happen right now. I cringed at my predicament and didn't know what to do.

I sat frozen in disbelief for another few minutes, then knew I had no choice but to summon my courage and confess my mistake to the mean manager and ask humbly if he would mind if I ran back to my apartment to get my wallet so I could pay.

To my surprise and relief, not only was he understanding, but he insisted I *not* return that day. He said not to worry about it—I could pay the next time I came in. He was so *not* mean about the situation (which he could have been), all I could say to him was, *"C'est très gentil.* Thank you so much for understanding."

In spite of his insisting that I pay at my convenience, I ran back home, grabbed my wallet, and ran back to pay anyway. As I handed him the money, he and I made direct eye contact and smiled at each other, calling an unspoken truce.

In a short time, Sabrina and I became friendly with everyone who worked at the café, the manager included, although he remained serious and distant. We were known as "Les Américaines," until one day we asked the servers their names, which surprised them and changed everything. There was Pablo, Lillia, and Chantal, who was pregnant. Lillia soon told us she was quitting to go work in an insurance agency in the neighborhood, which she had been hoping to be hired by for some time.

We introduced ourselves as well, and immediately thereafter, every morning we felt as though we were having breakfast with our friends instead of being strangers in a strange city.

It was a milestone for us, as making personal connections with Parisians had been one of our biggest challenges. Experiencing a sense of belonging, even if in such a small way, was a real victory. It also reinforced my belief that it's very easy to tell yourself stories about other people and believe them to be true, so much so that they become myths everyone buys into and reinforces. One of the myths I didn't want to buy into was that French people don't want to make friends with outsiders.

I'm not saying that French people aren't in the habit of being more insular and distant than Americans, because they are. But people are people, and we all appreciate being greeted with love and acceptance, no matter where we come from. And that was the myth I was choosing to live by.

Soon, every time we walked into "Cler" we were shown to "our" table, the same one by the window where we sat each morning. Our favorite new waiter, Aurélien, who replaced Lillia, would smile and say, *"Comme d'habitude?"* meaning "The usual?" before bringing us our usual order of café au lait and eggs. Then, if it was quiet, he would stay and chat with us about traveling the world, which he loved to do.

Now that we had a great place to live and had become anchored in the neighborhood at our new local café, the next thing we had to do to be officially settled in was to go to the French immigration office, or O.F.I.I., and get registered. This involved making an appointment on their website to get a physical examination at their location near the Bastille, to make sure we didn't have tuberculosis or some other communicable disease, which we promptly did.

Our appointment at O.F.I.I. was at 8 A.M. a few weeks later, and we were there bright and early, only to discover 200 other people also had 8 A.M. appointments. Apparently they had all gotten a secret memo saying 8 A.M. means 7:30 A.M., as when we showed up at 7:45, the line at the O.F.I.I. office was already around the block.

This was our first experience with French bureaucracy, and it was definitely an eye-opener. Once the doors opened at 8, we entered, one or two at a time, and presented our appointment papers to the woman at the front desk. From there we were told to take a seat in the now very crowded waiting room and wait until we were called.

There we sat for the next three and a half hours, waiting for our health exam. Once we were called, we had our vision checked, our heart rate measured, our balance checked, and finally were asked to disrobe from the waist up and have a chest X-ray. After that, and another long period in the waiting room, we were ushered in, one at a time, to see a woman doctor who put us on her exam table for about two minutes each, took our pulse, asked if we had had a recent tetanus shot, advised us to do so since we hadn't, and then gave us the okay to proceed. We were then sent back to the front and to yet another waiting area where, after sitting again for a time, we were finally called to the front desk. Our papers were processed, an official O.F.I.I. stamp was placed inside our passports, and we were set free to roam the streets of Paris in peace. Hurray! Success!

Walking out at 1:30 P.M., Sabrina and I high-fived each other as we examined the stamp. We were now officially processed immigrants, legally able to call Paris our home for the next full year, with a chance for renewal every year after that.

With my O.F.I.I. stamp in hand, nothing now stood in my way of finding new ground, a new sense of self, both inside and out. And the best part was that it was in *Paris!*

Summertime
on the Seine

Our new neighborhood opened us up to an entirely new set of discoveries as we soon found out on our regular nightly walks. We now considered ourselves "night walk–aholics" and couldn't relax without our daily fix of a two- or three-hour exploratory excursion in the evening after work and dinner.

As in the 18th, this new part of Paris invited us to seek out its treasures. Our best discovery was the walk along the left bank of the Seine, which came alive now that it was summer. The entire length of the river, from our apartment near the Eiffel Tower at avenue Bourdonnais all the way to the Louvre and beyond, had been turned into a summer playground, filled with bistros, floating restaurants, discos, picnic areas, art installations, and more.

Just near the point where we descended from the street overlooking the Seine to the river walk along its shore was Pont de l'Alma, where there was a flame-shaped monument to Princess Diana. It was just below this spot where she died on that fateful night in August 1997.

The monument was usually surrounded by bouquets of flowers, as well as odd mementos, photos, and letters to Diana left by tourists. I had noticed at the beginning of June that small locks suddenly started appearing on the railing surrounding the monument, with people's names and hearts written on them in permanent marker, left by lovers, young and old, who wanted to proclaim their undying love. They gravitated to Diana's monument because the bridge where the locks were formerly placed was at risk of falling into the Seine, it was so loaded with locks. The local authorities cut off all the locks and placed a plastic barrier in front of the railing. No further locks could be put there. Now the lovers' locks were popping up all around Paris, attestations of undying love not to be denied.

Isn't that what we all wish for, in the end? I said to myself, feeling lonely, as I noticed how quickly these locks accumulated. One evening, at the beginning of my walk, I was suddenly inspired to attach a small lock of my own on the railing as a commitment to my new love affair with myself.

I bought one from the conveniently located stand outside a local *tabac* on avenue Bourdonnais, just across from the bridge, and proudly attached it alongside the others.

Standing there reminded me just how quickly life can change—or worse, end—so I resolved that every time I passed by this spot, I would be grateful for my life, even with all its turbulence.

It was especially helpful to see this monument, and my little lock, when I was tempted to slip backward and start feeling sad and upset about the past. My heart was still in so much pain, but at the same time, I was grateful to be alive and well *in Paris*. Paris was healing too, from the terrorist attacks of only six months earlier. I admired the commitment to live fully and well that I saw bursting out everywhere I looked. It was teaching me something important.

Both by day and by night, the walk along the Seine became especially vibrant as we got deeper into summer, with tons of people, young and old, singles, couples, families, tourists, and groups of friends, all just hanging out in the endless array of cafés and playgrounds, enjoying the summer and each other.

I was completely enamored of the street performers, mimes, poets, singers, rappers, drummers, and dancers contributing to the festivity, each one as intent on being discovered as on making a buck.

One of my favorite spots to stop and enjoy the local talent was on the Pont Notre Dame, just behind Notre Dame, the second oldest bridge in Paris, leading to the Left Bank. Here I was entertained by some of the most quintessential French street performers to be had, my favorite being a local jazz ensemble of eightysomething-year-olds performing their hearts out every Sunday afternoon and evening, who no doubt had been doing the same for the past 50 years. Among the group, or alongside anyway, was a trippy, very eccentric, tiny *grande dame,* who appeared to be at least as old as the guys performing. She looked sublime with her deeply wrinkled face surrounded by a loosely pulled-up bun; bright red lipstick; rouged cheeks; and a long, red, almost featherless boa slung around her shoulders. She wore a ratty-looking dark-green velvet dress, colorful striped tights with holes in them, and well-worn jazz dance shoes. Lost in the music, she simply swayed in a dreamy bliss of her own. She had on the same outfit each time I saw her, and I got the impression that she had been their groupie since the beginning and would probably dance with them until she danced on out of here altogether. She was oblivious to the crowd, eyes closed, as she swung and swooned with the sax, spun and dipped with the main singer, and shuffled to and fro with an imaginary and obviously very good dance partner. I wanted to be like her, freely dancing my way through life, oblivious to the world around me. I wondered how she would feel if I joined her and swayed alongside her every time I passed by. I doubted she would even notice.

A little farther along the bridge, there was always the same old accordion player, sitting on his folding chair, playing "La Vie en Rose" for the tourists. I knew it was kitschy, but I loved him and his song, and stopped and listened for a while each time I passed by, leaving a few euros in gratitude for keeping the music alive in my heart.

It was especially intoxicating to visit this spot at night, when the streetlamps lit up and the reflection of the lights from the boats on the river sparkled on the water. With Notre Dame lurking in the background like a mysterious Gothic castle and soft clouds drifting overhead, this spot was one of the most beautiful in Paris and sprinkled magic dust all over my heart and soul every time I stood there.

The golden-pink light of Paris at night is hypnotic and seductive. This magical hue creates a sensuous glow that softens the hard, gray, sharp edges of the city and quietly calms the city as it wraps us all in its romantic allure. There is no other city in the world that casts such a spell, all because of this light. It softens the heart and lulls you into a dreamy, romantic state of mind.

You have to be willing to stay up pretty late, though, if you want to have the pleasure of such an experience in the summer. This is because Paris is so far north that it doesn't get dark until nearly 11 P.M. It was great. The long summer hours extended the day for us and allowed us to fully enjoy leisurely evening walks, even when we had to work late.

Walking in Paris at night lures you into an entirely new experience of the city. This feels especially true when walking on the Île Saint-Louis, the tiny island right behind Notre Dame that houses some of the oldest and richest residents in Paris, all nestled among quaint little bistros and tons of tourist shops. We had to stop at Berthillon for ice cream every time we strolled onto the Île. It was just the thing to do. And yes, all the tourists who had learned of this delicious spot from their many guidebooks were in line along with us, all of us like little kids patiently waiting to get our treat. But so were the Parisians. Everyone loved a *petit* Berthillon.

Walking along, night after night, I was also impressed by how resilient the French were, given the attacks of a few months ago. Everywhere I looked, life was going on full speed, and everyone seemed committed to enjoying life to the fullest in spite of the presence of young soldiers with their rifles strolling among us, reminding us of the ever-present danger of attack.

One of my favorite things to do on these nocturnal promenades was to peek into other people's homes. To my surprise, Parisians aren't particularly private when it comes to closing their curtains at night, at least in the summer, most likely because they probably need the cooler evening breeze because it's so hot. With a little neck craning, you can see quite a bit. One of the things we saw the most was naked Parisians in all shapes and sizes, parading around their apartments with no modesty whatsoever.

Here, a naked body is no big deal, as evidenced by the famous topless beaches in the south of France. And they're no longer limited to the south—if you can't get to the beach in Saint-Tropez, no worries. Every summer Paris brings the beach to itself, trucking in 5,000 tons of sand in the middle of July and actually creating two separate beaches along the Seine. Sabrina and I were just as likely to see nude sunbathers here on this artificial beach at noon as we were to see them on a beach in Saint-Tropez. And not just confident, twenty-something, gorgeous, young nude sunbathers either.

There were just as many older women as young babes catching a few rays. Everyone along the Seine seemed happy to let it all hang out; no one acted self-conscious about his or her body at all. That, too, was a totally refreshing break from our American obsession with youth and perfection.

Older women didn't seem to be on a timer here, as they so often were at home, dismissed and ignored once they hit a certain age. Lounging on beach chairs in the sand like regal tigers, they slathered suntan oil all over their exposed faces and chests, clear down to their waists, then turned their closed, relaxed eyes to the sun.

You go, girlfriends, I cheered them on silently as I walked by, too modest and too restless to lie in the sun alongside them. *More power and sunshine to all of you!*

Because I love to dance, I actually preferred the evening beach scene on the walk back from the Île Saint-Louis to the apartment, as it was rocking and rolling every night with local bands and DJs against the Paris moonlight. It was nonstop entertainment walking from one end of Paris to the other like this every night, and just strolling along felt as though we were attending great nightly parties. More than once we started spontaneously dancing under the moonlight as we strolled from band to band, when the music moved our souls.

It helped to have this built-in summer nightlife, as we still hadn't made any friends of our own yet, except of course Jean Luc, and it was tempting to feel sorry for ourselves in that department. As exciting as Paris was, we had not been there long, and truthfully I had not yet felt ready to begin meeting too many new people, so our social life was just the two of us.

Falling asleep after yet another long nightly walk, I reflected on how unsettled I still was despite the beauty around me. Moving to a new country liberates you from all that is outside of you, but what is inside remains, and being married for 32 years left a lot inside me. As much as I wanted to forget and move on, I was troubled by flashbacks of past family trips, Christmases, birthdays, and more that I couldn't stop from appearing. The memories were like ghosts following me around, but even worse were the feelings they carried. No matter how far I walked, they were right on my heels.

The biggest feeling chasing me around was questioning if I had made the right choice to just up and move. I was glad I was here, as it drew me out of the past. *But could I make a real life here?* I wondered. *With roots and community?* I had nothing to ground me, nothing to give just yet, so that seemed a long way from where I was.

I had the freedom to be whomever I wanted to be. No one knew me or expected anything of me. It was only my ingrained expectations that were holding me back, and shedding all these layers was my greatest need and challenge. They ran me like a perpetual motion machine.

In order to break these old ways of being, I had to stop myself again and again, get fully centered in my body, and really tune in to what *I* felt and wanted *today*. Whether it was what I wanted to eat for dinner or where I wanted to go for a walk or even what to wear (especially given the hard-core Parisian fashion expectations), it took me by surprise to realize that often my honest answer was "I don't know." It was a luxury to be able to seek these answers though and not have to worry about anyone else coming first.

Back to Basics

One of the ways we became grounded in Parisian life was that Sabrina cooked dinner for us every night. Going to the markets every morning on rue Cler and on rue Grenelle to buy fresh food for dinner became the central point of our day and an important ritual to help us feel like more than visitors. And with each daily visit to the various shops, we began to get to know and sort of make friends with the shopkeepers.

Or at least some of them. The young man at the greengrocer on rue de Grenelle developed a big crush on Sabrina and within a week he was offering her little gifts of apples and plums and radishes every time she came in. Soon the little gifts became bigger gifts, and she found herself coming home with an extra bag of fruit or vegetables each day. It got to be so much that she began to feel awkward going in there. I told Sabrina to just relax and enjoy the attention. I, for one, appreciated the bounty.

The women who worked at the *boulangerie* across the street, on the other hand, never seemed to recognize me even though I was there every morning like clockwork. Even so, they were always nice and sang, *"Bonjour, Madame"* out to me like morning songbirds, so it was a pleasant stop.

The cheese man next door was another situation altogether. He was so gruff and impatient, he was downright scary. The problem was that we couldn't avoid him—his cheese shop was simply the best in the neighborhood and only three minutes from our front door. Every time we went in, he would first ignore us for a while, then suddenly turn our way and shout, *"Dites-moi!"* which meant "Tell me," with an impatient shrug, as if we were holding him up from something urgent. We could never speak up fast enough for him. We wanted to ask about the different cheeses, but when we tried to ask, he brushed us off, so we pointed to whatever looked good and crossed our fingers, hoping we made the right choice. It was a hit-or-miss way to choose cheese, but we mostly had hits.

One day I asked innocently, "What is that cheese?" pointing to something that looked delicious. He immediately snapped back, "It is clearly marked, Madame, on the small sign in front of it. It is *fromage de chèvre,*" meaning "goat cheese." He was so unpleasant it occurred to me that maybe he didn't like Americans. But soon after that, I saw him be equally nasty to a French customer, so I realized he simply didn't like people, and his treatment of us was nothing to take personally. We started calling him the "Stinky Cheese Man" after that, like the character in one of Sabrina's and Sonia's favorite childhood books, quietly laughing under our breath every time we went in there and got ignored or yelled at. He reminded me all over again that customer service is simply not a given thing in the small shops in Paris. If the shop owner doesn't like you for whatever reason, you are simply out of luck.

Whether or not he liked me, I liked his cheese, so I steeled myself and went into his shop a few times a week. Was it worth it? With a *tradition,* as the traditionally made baguette is called; a freshly cut green apple, often gifted to Sabrina from the greengrocer; and his cheese, I was in heaven. So yes, it was.

Thanks to Sabrina's culinary skills, every night we had a feast. Her job was to cook; mine was to clean up after her. She was a very messy cook, so I figured our jobs were equal. These evening meals were the highlight of our day. They helped us settle in and calm our overreactive, anxious selves. We snapped at each other a lot while preparing for dinner, not only because of our Romanian blood, but also because we were a mother and daughter living together for the first time in more than seven years. But the minute we sat down to eat, we started laughing and toasting with a glass of red wine or mineral water and hugging each other, grateful for this new adventure we were sharing, never once holding a grudge.

One day we met Jean Luc in the hallway and asked if he heard our fights. He said yes, and then asked if we heard his. We also said yes, and we all laughed. Living in this building was like living in a quirky commune. There was Jean Luc's mother on the seventh floor, whom we saw only a few mornings a week as she ambled over to rue Cler with her cane to do her shopping. Then there was his sister, whom we were never formally introduced to, who lived on the third floor. We never saw her, but we did see her husband, as he was overseeing some of the work on the building.

Then there was the extended Iranian family above us, with all kinds of aunts and uncles visiting and celebrating one thing or another, as we could tell by the almost nightly sing-alongs and clapping overhead.

Below us lived a sad-looking single woman in her 50s, who several times rang our doorbell to tell us water was leaking from our apartment into hers. I let Jean Luc know this immediately, but he said to ignore her—she had been claiming this since she moved into the building more than 15 years earlier, and never once had a leak been found. Next door to her was a recent widow from Princeton, who had relocated to Paris with her five daughters in much the same spirit as we had, to recover from her severe loss and move on from the life she had before.

And, of course, there was also *Madame Gardien* and her husband, whom I had learned were from Portugal and were about to retire at the end of the year.

Once everyone acclimated to us, the greetings became a little warmer each time we saw one of the other tenants in the *rez de chausée*. Since the elevator was so small, there was a little game among us if we entered the building at the same time, as to who would ride up and who would walk. I always chose walking, but there were times when it was tempting to say, "My turn to ride." I never did, of course. That would be way too American and direct. I just figured walking up all these stairs would help burn off the croissants and fromage and support my commitment to have buns of steel.

I couldn't help but be constantly aware of just how much the mundane world dominated my attention right now, which wasn't at all like me. For most of my life I focused on the spiritual world, the unseen world, and paid far less attention to the physical realm.

Now I could see that this was because my physical world had been so predictable and grounded. I was always surrounded by my large family and my long-term friends. I knew my city and had lived in my neighborhood for years. I took all these things for granted. Now that I was in a new city with no community whatsoever, I realized how important these connections really are and how necessary it is to have these grounding elements in your life.

Here, life was reduced to waking up, meditating, shopping, cooking, cleaning, working, walking, and sleeping, all of which were time-consuming. Even doing laundry still required our full attention. And speaking of laundry, French clothes dryers are a complete ruse. They can hold only a very small load of laundry, and the cycle runs for three hours! It's unbelievable that anything needs that long to dry. And even after three hours, the laundry comes out damp. Nothing ever, ever comes out dry because the dryers aren't vented to the outside. The good news, however, is that in Paris, it is expected that all your laundry will be ironed— not only your shirts and pants and skirts, but also your kitchen and bath towels, sheets and bedding, and even your underwear. The damp state in which the laundry emerges is perfect for ironing out all the wrinkles. Too bad I couldn't do that with my life, although I did visualize doing just that every time I opened up the ironing board and got out the basket of damp laundry.

Getting back to basics in this way offered its own deep satisfaction. Because of the effort required to accomplish these fundamental tasks, we were forced to get back to the basics of life and stay present. We couldn't jump ahead, because each activity demanded time and attention. Each day's activities, though hardly lofty in aspiration, allowed for more intimacy with life, which in itself was a revelation.

Nothing we did, and no encounter with people, was automatic. In adapting to the culture, the language, the new living circumstances, and even the laundry, we were developing a keen ability to live in the present moment. All we could focus on most days was getting through each day and not thinking about tomorrow until tomorrow. Attending to these external essentials of daily life connected me to the internal essential in me.

Day by not-so-mundane day, the psychic walls that held the long-married me in place started to crumble. No part of married me fit here. The "caretaker," the "accommodator," the "problem solver," the "rescuer," the "self-sacrificer," the "overgiver," the "overachiever," the "overresponsible overworker," and, sad to say, the "resenter" that I was in my marriage just didn't seem relevant to my new situation. Like the broken chunks of cracked plaster being dragged out of the apartments above and below me as the building renovations continued, these obsolete identities were slowly being carried away as well.

I also realized that most of these worn-out patterns and personae hadn't originated in my marriage. They were formed way back in childhood and were part of the baggage I had brought into my marriage.

These parts of me, which I may have needed once upon a time in order to survive a big family and Catholic school, had long lost their usefulness and had now become a suffocating prison.

I had actually started breaking out of this prison before my divorce, before I walked the Camino the first time, and had been steadily sawing away at the invisible bars ever since. In Paris, I began to enjoy the first taste of freedom.

Monsieur Coupe

A "friend" on Facebook (whom I had never met in person and actually didn't know at all) enthusiastically wrote to me when she learned I had moved to Paris and insisted that I immediately book an appointment with a remarkably gifted (according to her) hairdresser who offered something called the *Coupe Énergique*, a haircut that she promised would be so amazing it would heal my life. Of course, I had to try it.

I arrived at a very tiny salon on the day of my appointment and was immediately ushered into a small stall of sorts and asked to sit and wait. Ten minutes later, the Coupe Énergique maestro himself, a small French man, walked in. He failed to say the prerequisite *"Bonjour, Madame,"* and instead immediately put on his eyeglasses and began examining my nearly shoulder-length hair very closely, as if it were attached to a dummy. He took it into his hands and brought it up to his eyeballs as he checked it out, nodding and *hmm*ing the whole while, barely acknowledging it was attached to a real person.

Finally, after several long minutes in which I was holding my breath, he took in a long, deep breath of his own, then sighed, stepping back as if to brace himself as he delivered the bad news.

"Madame," he said in heavily accented English, "I can see by the sadness in your hair that you have had some experience of great and deep trauma." I nearly burst into tears at this witnessing of my wounded self and nodded in agreement. *Finally, someone who understands me!* I thought.

Not wasting a moment, he continued, "I will now remove theez great trauma and set you free from theez terreeball past. Eet eez not po-seee-blah with such *baad* energy in your hair to live the life. You will not be good."

Worried by the gravity of his diagnosis, and grateful that he "got" what I had been through, I wholeheartedly agreed with him and said, "Please do," without having a clue as to *what* I was agreeing to have done in order to remove this "baad" energy.

A cape was draped around me. Next, he whipped out a long razor from a drawer just in front of us, put it in his left hand, grabbed a chunk of my hair with his right, and quicker than I could blink an eye, razored off my hair nearly to the scalp. I gasped in horror at what had just happened.

He patted me reassuringly and said, smiling, "Et voilà!" with smug self-satisfaction. "Zeee baad energy eez gone now." He then took another chunk off with a second razor whack. I sat frozen in shock and disbelief at what was happening, completely unable to protest. Besides, it was too late to stop him. He continued to gleefully whack and razor away, never once noticing the blood draining out of my face and quite possibly my entire head. In less than five minutes, all my hair was on the floor and he stood smiling at his work, looking as though he had just saved my life.

After congratulating himself loudly for what he clearly considered yet another successful rescue mission, he turned my chair away from the mirror and toward him and said in all confidence, "You will now be good." He then swiveled on one foot and began exiting the stall, stopping just before he was all the way out to turn back toward me for a final dramatic bow.

As he stepped out, he handed me off to a waiting shampoo girl, who reached out to me as if I were a mental patient who had just received shock therapy and needed to be treated with kid gloves. She was right. After what had just happened, I did. Shampoo Girl led me slowly over to the shampoo bowl, which was all of 10 feet away, whispering to me in French as I sat down in the chair how fortunate I was to have been able to see "Le Monsieur" as soon as I had, as he had a waiting list of over two years. She then swished some sweet-smelling shampoo throughout what little of my hair remained, reviving me from the stunned state I was in, telling me this would remove the final negative vibrations. She gave me a good head massage, then rinsed my hair with a brisk dose of cold water and toweled it dry. When she finished, she removed the hair towel and combed through my shorn locks, saying I didn't need a blow dry, or "brushing" as they call a blow dry in France, as I had so little hair left, it would dry naturally in just a few minutes. *No shit,* I thought, barely holding back my tears. There was no point.

She then went to fetch my coat, and a moment later returned with both it and a bill for 200 euros for my professional scalping. She then told me that I also needed the special shampoo she had just used on me as a post "coupe" follow-up to clear any residual bad energy and cut any remaining cords to the past. This she quickly put in a bag and handed to me before I could decline, adding that it would be another 40 euros.

Shell-shocked, I paid. Just as I did, Monsieur Coupe appeared once again, as if on cue, in case I wanted to thank him before I left. Being polite, of course, as well as completely stunned, I did. As I walked down the street in a daze, *still* wanting to be a believer, I tried to tell myself that this was the best thing that could have happened to me. That is, until I saw myself in the reflection of a store window. Reality then kicked in hard. I looked like a scalped poodle.

Knowing there was nothing I could do about it, I just kept walking, wondering if Monsieur Coupe removed old trauma by simply inflicting new trauma to replace it. Every time I looked over and saw my reflection, I wanted to cry. With each step I kept hoping my hair would somehow suddenly bounce back, telling myself it just needed a few minutes to relax, and it wasn't that bad.

I had arranged to meet Sabrina at Cler after my appointment. One look at me and her eyes bulged out in shock.

"What have I done to myself?" I cried, bursting into the tears I had been fighting back. "I cannot believe I allowed this to happen."

Sabrina tried to reassure me. "It's not *that* bad. And, who knows, Mom? Maybe this *is* exactly what you need in order to move on."

I calmed down and eventually showed her the shampoo, and we both burst out laughing.

Resolved to make the best of it, I decided that rather than feel regret, I would believe that it *was* the best thing that happened to me and that the hair I lost *was* full of bad vibes and pain. I couldn't help but wonder, however, how I could avoid having my new hair be filled with the same painful energy, given how I felt about this haircut at the moment.

There were two big lessons to be learned in all of this: first, the pain of the past is unfortunately not so easily stripped away, and second, not to allow anyone ever again to take a literal or figurative whack at me.

Playing Dress-Up

Walking around Paris, I often saw lovers throw themselves into each other's arms with abandon, kissing each other madly in the middle of the street or on a bridge over the Seine, losing themselves in their ardor, oblivious to the world around them. I felt jealous that this was not happening to me.

I felt like a voyeur, longing for that same passion in someone's arms, and feared it would never be mine again. There were days when I struggled with the feeling that I had wasted my life, remaining way too long in a marriage that wasn't working, and worried that it was now too late, or that I was too old, to ever have the kind of deep, comforting love and companionship I so yearned for and honestly felt I'd never fully had.

The battle between my head and heart sometimes got ugly. There were days when I genuinely believed I'd never be in love again. The quiet answer from the Universe was always, *Just fall in love with yourself, Sonia. It is time.*

Sabrina struggled with the same fears and challenges as I did. We took turns dumping our fears on the table and hashing them out over our morning café au lait, our egos sometimes competing for the floor. We found the only way to manage all this internal anxiety was to keep filling the empty well within us with larger and larger doses of positive self-talk, daily exchanges of mutual support, praying, taking in the beauty all around us, eating delicious food, drinking occasional glasses of champagne, and—guess what else?—shopping!

Day after day, we found ourselves drawn like bears to honey into one gorgeous Parisian boutique after another. We tried on fabulous clothes and shoes, some so over-the-top we laughed out loud at the extravagance of it all. Playing dress-up like this became our favorite summer game, as we shamelessly went into every glamorous store that beckoned and tried on everything we loved but could never, *ever* afford.

Our favorite place to indulge our lust for luxury was avenue Montaigne, where all the famous designer houses were lined up one after another, making it easy: Chanel, Dolce & Gabbana, the House of Dior, Yves Saint Laurent, Nina Ricci, Prada, Givenchy, Manolo Blahnik, and more. There were so many designer boutiques along this strip, it made our heads spin. We got high on our fashion escapades.

Each time we went into one of these glamorous fashion houses, we immediately engaged the salespeople by complimenting the store, openly and unabashedly admiring the clothes, and telling them how much we absolutely loved everything on display, including them. Then we asked the super serious salespeople if we could try some things on.

It worked every time. In only moments, their solemn facades fell to the floor and they began to play along with us. Like kids going through a costume box, we asked to try on this and that, and don't forget the tiara while you are at it. Squealing with delight as we tried on gowns and dresses and shoes and sunglasses and hats and sometimes what felt like downright crazy costumes, we had a blast. Our fun was contagious, and inevitably the more fun we had, the more the staff at the store wanted in on the fun as well. In no time, more salespeople drifted our way, offering us champagne, espresso, or sparkling water just to watch, if nothing else.

One thing I did notice is that most of the women who worked in these boutiques wore white button-down shirts and black blazers. I told them I bought one that didn't feel good so I gave it away, which surprised them. *"Il faut le chemise blanche,"* they all insisted, saying it was an absolute fashion staple in Paris. I promised I would try one again. They knew we wouldn't buy in their expensive boutiques but were nevertheless invested in us looking good in Paris, which was caring of them.

Soon, to our shock, the salespeople began to sweep us into their private showrooms where only the most exclusive clients would be invited, and let us try on their most outrageously expensive things. We got crazy with the staff at several boutiques, taking photos of each other and selfies together and pretending to walk the runway as we strutted around, never once spending a dime. On several occasions, we actually got drunk on fun.

We never went into these stores during their busy times, like on Saturdays, as we knew that was when the sales staff had to hustle to make their commissions, and we would only be a distraction. Instead we went in during the week, in the morning, when the stores were as dead as doornails, no shoppers in sight, and everyone stood around stifling yawns and looking bored to no end. That is when we took them by storm.

This was such a delicious way to chase the blues away, and since it was free, it wasn't dangerous. We left our credit cards at home so the temptation to buy in the moment would not overwhelm our common sense.

Even though we never purchased anything, we began to receive invitations to their *soirées*, meant just for their special, high-end clients. While we were flattered to receive them, we never did make it to any of these parties. It was enough just to be invited. We assumed they wouldn't be very fun anyway, because the super-rich *clientèle* would probably be snobby and reserved. We preferred our private dress-up parties to these more formal affairs. After one of our increasingly legendary visits, one of our new-found boutique friends, Sara, told us that most shoppers try on things but don't buy because it is too expensive for French people to afford what they sell. She said most of the clothes and shoes and accessories in the stores were bought by rich Arabs and Russians, and the rest of the people did what we did, only they were not as much fun or as honest as we were about it. She said they loved our American outrageousness and wanted to know if we were from

New York or Los Angeles because that was where they all wanted to go one day.

This made us laugh and feel relieved at the same time. After all, we were never certain if we were overstepping their boundaries by entering these boutiques just for fun. It was a surprise that so many of the salespeople we met were so willing—even happy—to play along with us.

More than the outrageousness of the clothes, it was the simple joy of playing dress-up that lifted my spirit and made me remember who I was. Since the divorce, I had not had much chance to laugh and be silly, and it felt good to have moments like these again.

Sadly, my divorce left me feeling full of self-doubt and more than a little shame. I knew this was just another facet of deep healing that my soul was now ready to embrace, but shame is tough to shake, and being clear that I was on my soul path and that my life journey was unfolding as it should was not enough to wipe away the sickening feeling inside me.

Dressing ourselves in such gorgeous gowns celebrated our femininity and snubbed these inner shaming indictments. The clothes were only props, supporting a much deeper liberation in our souls. We didn't need the clothes. But we did need the celebration.

Sabrina was the perfect playmate for these excursions. She had no problem asking to try on dresses that were $20,000 or more and parading around the store, laughing and enjoying the experience to the hilt. "Why not?" she would say, to which the staff would agree. "These gowns are made to be worn, not just hang on a hanger." She did more for my shattered and battered feminine self-esteem than anyone on these playdates.

Donning all these bejeweled gowns lifted me right out of the doldrums and helped me feel beautiful inside and out once again.

All of this fashion fun also helped distract us from the emotional void we had both felt since ending our relationships. We had both been involved in committed relationships for most of our adult lives, so not being partnered took some getting used to. Being alone made it clear to me just how much the expectation of being connected to a man had been imprinted on my psyche from the earliest age.

I was also made acutely aware of just how much I feared being judged (or perhaps judging myself) for *not* being in a relationship with a man, as if I was somehow not okay, or incomplete, or some sort of female outcast because of it. I never consciously thought I *needed* to be with a man to feel good about myself. But then again, I had been in one relationship or another since I was 16 years old, so how could I have known?

I knew in the depth of my soul that it was time for me to banish all of this patriarchal nonsense once and for all. If I were to experience any true, long-lasting emotional freedom and happiness and peace as a woman, it could only come about by my getting to the place inside me where I was filled with so much self-love that I considered any relationship with a man to be a bonus, not a necessity. I desperately wanted to get to this place and fast. The only problem was that I couldn't rush this process no matter how hard I was trying to. I just had to be patient as I shed these old, tiresome, soul-deadening layers and fall in love with me.

En Vacances

I had heard that many Parisians go on vacation for the month of August, but I had no idea that it meant almost the entire city would close down and empty out.

Apart from the main tourist attractions, which remained open no matter what, most places in Paris turned the lights out and left a note on their front door that said *En vacances,* meaning "On vacation"—essentially, "See you in September." This included, of course, all of our favorite spots to eat and shop, leaving us irrationally feeling as though we had just been abandoned.

At first we decided we would make the best of this quiet time in the city, as Paris had been so jam-packed with tourists the month before that it left us feeling as though we had been invaded. Some Parisians love Paris in August, and I can understand why. The weather is beautiful, and without the crowds you feel as though you have the city all to yourself.

But the feeling of living in a ghost town took us by surprise and we didn't like it.

We decided to go to Florence, and immediately set about finding a place to stay on Airbnb. With that mission accomplished, we packed our bags and took a quick one-hour flight for only 100 euros. It was exciting to be able to get so easily to another wonderful European destination and we counted that as another positive of living in France.

The change of scenery and temperament in Italy was refreshingly warm and fun. We dove into large bowls of delicious homemade pasta; drank gallons of Italian espresso and chianti; and visited all the fabulous museums in town, including the Uffizi Gallery, with its wonderful collection of old masters Botticelli, Fra Angelico, Leonardo da Vinci, and hundreds more, and the Accademia Gallery, where we were left stunned by the incredible statue of David by Michelangelo.

We strolled through the small winding streets and along the river and returned again and again to Brunelleschi's majestic and mind-boggling Cathedral of Santa Maria del Fiore, pondering how on earth these Renaissance geniuses managed to create such masterful works of art and architecture without any modern technology.

The food, the art, and the cafés were all so wonderfully uplifting that, in spite of the massive crowds (I honestly think the entire city of Paris and all the rest of Europe had emptied itself here), we had a fabulous 10-day *vacances* of our own.

I could see why it was important to get away from Paris for a bit. While I was now falling very much in love with my new hometown, it was like falling in love with a moody, good-looking boyfriend who cooks really well, as my friend Anita pointed out to me one day. While I was fascinated and fully engaged, it was nice to get away from all the work of understanding a complicated, somewhat demanding city and just relax for a minute. Maybe Parisians felt the same way about themselves. Who knows?

At the same time as we were enjoying our sojourn in Florence, however, a very disturbing event was taking place across Europe, and it was heartbreaking to witness and absorb. Millions of people from the Middle East, including and especially from Syria, where people were risking their lives to escape the horror of civil war and invasion by the Islamic State, were paying massive sums of money to be smuggled to Europe in far too overloaded, unseaworthy boats.

It was shocking to see this mass exodus happening so close to our new home. In the U.S., people watched all of this on this news but could easily ignore or tune it out because it was so far removed from their day-to-day world. Here in Europe, however, it was impossible to ignore because it was happening in our back-yard. It was an immigration disaster that dominated news and conversations in every country. There were daily reports of entire families—men, women, and children—drowning in the Mediterranean Sea. It was so tragic, only the most hardened could tune it out.

Germany took a stand, perhaps to help heal their own horrific past, and opened their doors to accept as many immigrants as they could, and with that announcement, more than a million refugees began pouring into Europe.

Some countries didn't respond as hospitably as Germany, even though it seemed the only humane thing to do, as this was the biggest refugee exodus since World War II. But it was all so complicated, as many people feared that along with the refugees, radical Islamist terrorists from Syria would slip in and launch attacks on the innocent and unsuspecting public. Then there was plain old xenophobia showing its face, as well. Some countries just didn't want their culture infiltrated by outsiders and made that perfectly and hostilely clear.

It wasn't all bad. Millions of generous people across Europe opened their hearts and homes to the refugees and demonstrated the power of love. They stood along the roads handing food, clothing, water, shoes, and more to the waves of migrants as they trudged for miles and miles, trying to get to Germany, or farther, in sweltering heat. Being in Europe offered us firsthand experience in observing both the extreme light and shadow of the human race, watching people who wanted to help and heal and others who were fearful and divided and who hardened their hearts toward these people.

There were entire refugee families now living on the streets, with babies and small children in tow, all seated on a single piece of cardboard with small signs saying "refugee" or "Syrian family, please help" in French, English, and Arabic.

Back in Paris, we were horrified to witness the plight and suffering of these people, many now huddled together along rue de Grenelle or near the École Militaire, just steps from our doorstep.

Sabrina and I didn't know what to do, so we went to a sporting-goods store called Decathlon and bought tiny lightweight sleeping bags and handed them out. We also bought sandwiches from the boulangerie and bottles of water to dispense. It seemed like such a paltry effort given how much the refugees needed. But it felt better than walking past them or handing them only money (which we also did).

We called several refugee organizations and asked if we could help, but they required a commitment of uninterrupted time, which I was unable to give due to my work travel schedule. So we just kept giving out sleeping bags and food and money to the people we walked past and made donations to the organizations that did help.

The summer refugee crisis hit my heart like a bullet and cracked it open. The relentless waves of suffering people walking across Europe in the blistering heat to get to safety, only to be treated like animals in some cases, boggled my mind.

Rather than simply be appalled and blame the inhumane behavior of others for causing all this horror, however, I knew that unless I chose to become part of the solution, I, too, would bear responsibility for perpetuating the problem. This was a world problem, and it wasn't going to just go away.

I felt a renewed commitment to step up and love others more deeply, more generously, and more unconditionally than ever before. How could I rally for peace and at the same time still harbor anger and bitterness of any sort in my own heart? As easy as it would be to separate the two, I couldn't. Deep in my gut I knew the negativity I still harbored within me and the negativity in the world around me were all connected, even if I couldn't always see the lines connecting the dots directly.

To help bring peace to the world and ease the cause of the horrors I was seeing, I had to own my part in perpetuating hate and ignorance. I had to clear all the places in my own heart and mind where I still held on to anger and hurt, all the places in my life where I held myself aloof from others, all the places where I lacked compassion or felt self-righteous indignation or was judgmental or stayed addicted to pain—and that included my feelings toward my old life.

I knew I shouldn't expect this to miraculously occur, and that to have such demanding expectations only set me up for failure, but I did know that in my heart and spirit I truly didn't want to live short of this. I wanted to be a genuinely healed, open-hearted person in the world so I could help others find their way to this clarity as well.

Day after day, watching more and more desperate people stream out of the Middle East toward relative safety, I wondered if this was in fact the soul assignment all humans were being asked to undertake now. I felt the call in my heart. And I was ready to answer it.

La Rentrée

September came and Paris sprang back to life. Parisians began pouring back into the city, turning on their lights, and opening the doors to their shops and restaurants once again, looking seriously suntanned (no sunblock for these people), feeling refreshed and ready to tackle *la vie* once again.

Since it was back-to-school time, I felt ready to take some classes myself. I decided to enroll in some yoga and boxing classes. Despite all the walking I did, I had eaten enough pasta and ice cream over the past month that I had a hard time squeezing into my clothes, so I realized it was time to get back *en forme,* as they say in French.

My first search was for a yoga studio. To my delight I found one only five minutes from our apartment that offered all styles and levels of yoga classes from morning to night, six days a week. It was perfect. Since the classes were all in French, it would double as a language lesson of sorts, as I would need to understand what the instructor was saying.

The owner of the studio was a welcoming American ex-pat named Oliver who had lived in France for many years, so the enrollment part was a breeze. With his encouragement and my enthusiasm, I quickly signed up for an unlimited monthly subscription. As I planned on being there every morning, bright and early, the price seemed like a bargain.

After searching through my stuff, I found my yoga clothes and mat and was ready to dive in to the 7 A.M. class the next morning.

I was pretty good at yoga before I quit practicing, so I had no hesitation in choosing an intermediate class for my own *rentrée* experience.

When I arrived the next morning, I expected to be greeted by a smiling, good-looking, enthusiastic yoga instructor swaying to upbeat music, as was the case in my American yoga classes. Instead, the small room was absolutely silent and packed with very solemn, mostly middle-aged or older French women, staring blankly ahead and avoiding eye contact with anyone at all costs. Mat in hand, I had to maneuver around the group to find my own few inches of space; not a single woman moved over to accommodate my arrival. Trying several times to fit my mat into a spot to no avail, I ended up in the corner, with just enough space for most of my mat and not an inch more.

Namaste to you, too, I thought, annoyed with the complete lack of friendliness and warmth.

After a few more minutes, a very somber-looking French woman of about 45 entered the class and, without saying a word, rang a small bell and signaled the class to begin. The next thing I knew, I was up and down and bumping into the other women every which way as I tried to understand and follow the instructor—and her French—as she flew through the postures. In no less than 10 minutes I had managed to smash into three other students and poke one woman in the eye with a fling of my arms, huffing and puffing to keep up, with no help from the instructor whatsoever. If anything, she seemed annoyed with me, as did the other students.

After a few more failed attempts to keep up, let alone understand what the heck the instructor was saying, she suddenly stopped the class and walked over to me. Without smiling, she asked me if I had ever taken yoga before. When I said yes, she raised an eyebrow that clearly indicated she didn't believe me. She then said that this was an *intermediate* class and beyond my level. The women in the class seemed to join her in raising their eyebrows at me as well, letting me know that they also did not appreciate me disrupting *their* class with my ineptitude. She then asked me to sit out the rest of the class and begin at my *proper* level the next time.

Felling humiliated, I retreated back to my corner and began to sit down, when she stopped me with a *"Non! Pas là!"* meaning, "No, not there," and pointed to a spot in the front of the room nearly out the door. *"Là!"* she said, like a drill sergeant. I got up and obediently scrambled over like a kid in trouble in the class.

Well, this is a relaxing way to start the day, I thought as I rolled up my mat and left 10 minutes later, racing to get out the door as fast as I could, pissed that I had just paid for a month of this abuse, wanting never to return. Just before I escaped out the door, however, the instructor came up behind me and said in French, "Madame, I will see you tomorrow at the eight A.M. class. It's better for you."

I said, *"Merci, Madame. À demain,"* meaning, "Thank you. I'll see you tomorrow." And I knew I would.

Walking out, I felt demoralized. After a café au lait at Café Cler just around the corner, I regrouped and decided that I was being too sensitive and had to stick it out, at least for the month I paid for.

The instructor was right. I had overestimated my ability, both in understanding French at this fast pace and in my yoga practice. This was no time to let my ego interrupt my plan to get into shape once again. I just had to remind myself that people did things differently over here, and I needn't take it personally. I wasn't in America and had no right to expect the class to be like an American class.

Up again and ready to go the next day, I arrived 10 minutes early to secure my place on the floor. The minute the room opened up, I walked in and grabbed a spot right in front of where the instructor would be. That way I could better follow both her yoga instructions and her French. Shortly thereafter a few other women filed into the room with their mats and, like yesterday, plopped themselves down and silently stared straight ahead. It felt as if we were in a cross between military school and church. I decided to just observe and learn and hopefully enjoy my experience more today.

The instructor walked in exactly on time and once again rang the little bell. We started with 10 minutes of deep breathing and gentle stretches and slowly moved on to the postures. I followed along easily enough today, and there were fewer students in this class, so I had more room to move.

It wasn't fun, but it was nevertheless good for my body to start the day moving and stretching like this. Being here also underscored, once again, the difference between Americans and the French. We are often like enthusiastic, rambunctious puppies, jumping and bopping and noisily playing; at least in this class, they felt like snooty old cats, far more reserved, aloof, and "cool."

Besides this morning class being a good opportunity to learn French and yoga, it was also a good way to observe French women in action. Up until now I had not really been around too many French women. I hadn't made any true French friends yet, and apart from Jean Luc and the people who worked at Café Cler, I was either alone or with Sabrina most of the time, so this was new.

I could tell "friendly" yoga was not really the thing here. The women not only didn't smile at me, they also didn't smile at one another. It seemed to be a far more serious business here than I was used to.

I knew I was being judgmental, which I didn't want to be. I guess underneath it all I was hoping to connect with others as well as do yoga. Obviously that wasn't going to happen here, which disappointed me. *Oh well.*

Because yoga was a social bust, I also decided to enroll in a kickboxing class, which I had taken years earlier. At that time, I accidently kickboxed myself into a broken kneecap, but it had since healed and I was missing the fun and sport of it. Sabrina was also very interested in kickboxing classes, as she had taken them for years back in Los Angeles and missed them a lot.

I looked on the Internet and found a gym that specialized in boxing near the Palais Royale, and we went right over. It was a very small, very hip spot, and the guy who worked there spoke

English very well and was super welcoming. He said they taught two styles of boxing at this gym, English and French, and lessons were offered both individually as well as in groups. Of course, individual lessons would be much more expensive, he said, but group lessons could be a little intense, as they really go for the boxing part of kickboxing. He also said we had to pay a membership fee to join the gym no matter what classes we took. I asked if we could try one session before we committed to joining the gym. He said no, they had a policy that required you to join before you could try.

"But," he continued, "you could join for only a month, and after that discontinue your membership if you don't like it."

Sabrina was gung-ho on joining, so we did. She could hardly wait to have a personal lesson and signed up for one the next day. I had to wait until the weekend before I could take one myself, as they had lessons at my level (which I now respected and did not overrate) only at night.

We left feeling excited, as the place had a great vibe to it. It was less than a year old, with a very Zen-chic décor, and had a small café inside where members congregated after class, which also really appealed to us. Maybe we could make friends here.

While Paris was beautiful and exciting and endlessly interesting, the emotional connections we craved, apart from those little ones we experienced at Café Cler, or seeing Jean Luc once in a while, were not happening yet. Maybe this crazy little spot would change that.

Sabrina got dressed for class and set off immediately for her lesson at 6 the next evening, while I stayed home and worked a bit longer. She came back at 8, and when I asked how it had gone, she said it was "different." Of course it would be. Everything is. When I asked her how it was different, she said the instructor was very serious and not at all warm, but she liked her session and felt she got a good workout.

Knowing what she meant, I was nervous that this would be another disappointment. Sabrina assured me that she thought it wouldn't be and said we needed to give the place a chance.

The next day she left again at 6 P.M., this time for her group class. When she came back home she was visibly shaken and furious. Surprised, I asked her what had happened. She told me that in the group class, another student kept hitting her in the head, so she had to keep kicking her to back off. The class was like a *real* boxing match and not the fun workout she had expected at all. Now Sabrina is actually quite good at boxing, so she was no lightweight when it came to taking care of herself. But never in all of her years had she been boxed about the head in any class.

Sabrina was really disappointed and thought boxing was out for good, but my intuition told me to just keep on looking for a place that was right for us. After a few days of searching, I came across another boxing gym that was called the Belle Équipe, near the Gare du Nord. I loved the name and instantly felt that this would be *our* gym. We set out for it the next morning before work. We arrived at a magnificent French building located in the 10th arrondisement, the front door flanked by beautiful five-foot stone angels on either side. This was a good sign.

Once inside, we were greeted by the most delightful, funny, English-speaking, five-foot-five French guy named Rémy, and his less-fluent-in-English, six-foot-three partner, Julien. We told them about our experience at "Zen Boxing," at which they immediately rolled their eyes and said, "Ah, *non*. Eet's not for you."

We agreed. It wasn't. But instantly we felt *they* were. We both signed up immediately, very excited to have found our place. We started with separate lessons. Sabrina mostly worked with Rémy, who was a little more intense in his training, and I worked with Julien, who gave me a good workout but didn't break my back or knee or hit me in the head.

Working out with Rémy and Julien was incredibly fun for both of us. Twice a week, these guys seemed genuinely happy to see us. During our lessons they asked us questions about being here and gave us tons of advice about where to go to shop, to have coffee, and more. They showed interest in my work and ordered the French version of the books I wrote and acted more and more like genuine friends. It was a big leap into a more personal experience of Paris and anchored us here in an entirely new way.

I continued on with "solemn" yoga every morning, as it was easy to get to, and went to boxing classes twice a week in between.

The past year I had been in a relentless "tear down the old me" phase. Being in yoga and now boxing classes, with the new apartment as my foundation, I finally began to feel as though I was beginning to build myself back up again, spiritually as well as physically.

With Rémy and Julien's help, I started looking forward to what was new and exciting ahead. I was beginning to feel as though I was slowly waking up from a long and painful dream. It was more than my hope and my prayer; it was becoming a reality.

November 13th

By late October, our life in Paris had eased into a flow and with the changing colors of the leaves amid Indian summer temperatures, everywhere felt absolutely beautiful. But it was also the time of year when I had to go back and forth from Paris to the U.S. several times, as I had many workshops and conferences to teach.

Both of my daughters assisted me in these workshops, so Sabrina packed up with me and we set off first to Chicago. There we united with Sonia, and the three of us hunkered down into work mode.

After completing the last in a series of three intensive workshops in Chicago, traveling back and forth from Paris each time, I was scheduled to stop in Boston on November 13th to present at a conference on the way back to Paris. Sabrina didn't want to go. She had *finally* begun making some good friends in Paris, and one of them was having a birthday party on the same day as the conference. So she elected to return to Paris while I went on to Boston.

As soon as I landed and got into my rental car to drive out to the venue, I got an urgent text from Sabrina saying that there had just been another terrorist attack in Paris very near the party she was attending. The entire city was in lockdown, and everyone was glued to the television.

"I'm okay, Mom, but it's awful. I am so scared and just want to get back to our apartment, but can't. We are not allowed to go outside."

At first I was confused by what she was saying, then relieved that she was safe, and totally shocked and heart-sickened that terror had struck Paris again. I switched on the radio in my car to listen to the news, only to hear of the continuing horror unfolding in real time. Terrorists attacked the stadium where a soccer game was going on, along with several restaurants and cafés, one of which was called the Belle Équipe. Upon hearing this I panicked. I just heard "Belle Équipe" and not "restaurant," and for the life of me, I couldn't fathom why the terrorists would attack my boxing gym. I feared for Julien and Rémy.

Sabrina called 30 minutes later. She was whispering and I could tell she was shaken to her core. She said everyone in the city was told not to go outside until the police gave clearance. She felt trapped with all these strangers and just wanted to get home. I had a clearer idea of what was happening than she did, as she was afraid to use her phone too much for fear she would run out of juice and have no way of recharging it. She couldn't fully follow the French news that was on the television but saw enough to be sickened. I didn't share any of the news I had gathered with her as I didn't want to cause her further alarm.

What I had learned was that in addition to the cafés and the restaurants that had been attacked, a packed nightclub called the Bataclan, where a concert was going on, had been taken over by several armed terrorists, and there was a massive killing spree going on inside.

As I drove, I prayed out loud in gratitude that Sabrina was safe. Getting my head around these attacks was very difficult to do. Terror had never hit this close to home, and my brain kept trying to reject what it was learning. It seemed as if a surreal movie were unfolding across the ocean, in my new home, close to my daughter, and I was only able to observe this horror from afar.

Shortly thereafter, my phone starting going crazy, with friends and family calling to make sure Sabrina and I were safe and to scream at me to get us out of Paris and fast. My e-mail blew up with the same sentiments.

Sabrina eventually finagled a ride home with a guy she had just met at the party. He had a car and said he was leaving. She instantly grabbed his sleeve and begged, "Please, take me home too." He was drunk enough to agree and she was panicked enough to go with him. They snuck out of the party, not knowing what to expect once in the car, but thankfully the streets were absolutely abandoned, even police cars were nowhere in sight, so he flew all the way across Paris without being stopped, and miraculously, by 3:30 in the morning Paris time, Sabrina was safely home. She was certain that this guy was an angel and had been there for her. She called me the minute she walked in the door. Up until that point, every time I heard from her she was unnaturally calm. Once home, she fell apart.

Crying, she said she wanted to get out of Paris as soon as she could—she didn't want to be there alone. Since we had friends in Zagreb, Croatia, Sabrina booked a flight there the next day at 2 P.M.

She left Paris and I returned. When I arrived the city was stunned, shut down, and in mourning. Everyone looked as though they were in shock. It was a sorrowful feeling. Walking through the streets to get a few things at the market, people barely spoke to one another.

Friends of mine from Chicago had just arrived with their two college-aged kids the day before the attacks to attend a scheduled U2 concert, only to be greeted by its cancellation.

I met them at their hotel the evening I returned. Their heads were spinning. My friend's daughter had been considering studying abroad in Paris the following year, and this was part of the reason they had come, but with this event she had lost all interest.

I was saddened to hear this, but I understood. At the moment Paris was not the beautiful city of her imagination anymore. It was a bloodied and traumatized war zone, where going to a concert or sharing a drink at a local café cost people their lives. All we could do was shake our heads at one another in confusion. We struggled to take it in.

They cut their trip short and left the next day. I walked around the city and tried to absorb what had just happened. An intense show of police and military might was everywhere. I was both glad and sad to see it.

Living in Paris became more complicated with this latest atrocity. While friends and family kept asking when I was coming "home," the thought never occurred to me. This was my home now.

After the three days of mourning, it was as if an invisible curtain lifted. The city exploded with festive holiday lights, illuminating street after street, especially along the Champs-Elysées. There, starting from a huge red, white, and blue illuminated Ferris wheel at the place de la Concorde and continuing up to the *rond-point,* was one of the most beautiful, festive Christmas markets in the world. Vendors from all over France lined each side of the Champs-Elysées, 160 different little authentic chalets in all.

There were stalls selling every kind of French Christmas specialty treat imaginable. There were hot spiced wine bars; shops for sweet donuts, breads, Andouille sausage, and many types of country pâtés; cafés, oyster and champagne bars, beer and brats stands, and tons more.

These food shops were nestled in between shops that sold hats and rugs and Christmas lights and toys for kids and holiday arts and crafts from all around France. There were also silly rides and games for the kids, men dressed up in Saint Nicholas suits handing out candy, musicians performing and singing songs, and rides for the entire family. It really created a winter wonderland.

What struck me most was just how resilient the Parisians were. In absolute defiance of what had just happened, the Christmas market was packed with people. While there were as many police and military people carrying rifles strolling along the market as there were families with children, among the crowd there was an unshakable commitment to celebrating and enjoying life instead of cowering indoors in fear.

If there ever was a moment when I deeply appreciated this being called the City of Light, it was now. The spirit of this beautiful city and these people was not to be stolen. Everyone was deeply shocked and wounded beyond words, to be sure—but not defeated. If anything, the commitment to turning up the light became even stronger.

In the background of all this festivity, a massive manhunt was under way for the remaining suspects in the attacks. Meanwhile, the endless bright lights lifted our hearts and soothed the rawness we all felt inside. The juxtaposition epitomized the worst and best that human beings had to offer.

I visited the market several times leading up to Christmas, as there was so much to explore and enjoy and distract from the horror that still hung in the background. When Sabrina returned from Croatia, we decided to buy a Christmas tree and decorate our apartment. We selected a two-foot tree that was standing outside the florist's shop two blocks from our apartment. The owner of the shop, a gay Indian man, was so sweet and supportive that he closed the shop and personally carried our little tree all the way to our front door, throwing in the gift of a fresh wreath and some Christmas greens for the table.

It seemed that he, like most everyone else in Paris right now, had had his heart cracked open and felt the need to connect to people on a deeper than usual level. We felt it too. We asked him to join us for a holiday glass of champagne, which he gladly accepted, and before we knew it, several hours had passed.

As we sipped champagne, Arun told us how the flower shop was his pride and joy, yet so very difficult to keep open, as traffic was slower than he had imagined it would be. We encouraged him to believe in his dream and suggested that he pray for abundance.

He was Indian, but he was not at all religious or spiritual and said so. He was gay and his traditional Hindu parents did not accept him, which broke his heart. In response he decided to turn his back on them and his religion as well. Still, he delighted in our home, with its altars and spiritual icons from all over the world, and wondered if he had made a mistake with this decision since he found our spiritual atmosphere comforting.

I gave him a French edition of one of my books on listening to intuition, which he seemed overjoyed to receive. He left with enthusiastic French cheek kisses passed all the way around, all three of us feeling a reassuring sense of human connection and goodness in spite of the insanity that had just passed through our beautiful city.

After getting the tree, we visited the Christmas market again, this time in search of lights and decorations for both it and our apartment. We found so many kinds of lights at the market, it was amazing. We chose ones in the shape of stars in honor of the people who had just lost their lives. We strung them around the tree, across the fireplaces, and around the doors and windows so they lit up the entire apartment. As we decorated, we played holiday music, said prayers, and sang out loud with the intention to usher in positive love and light. Although Paris had just become a lot more complicated and even scary, it was now home, and we were committed to lighting it, and our lives, up with love. We needed it.

When we finished decorating, Sabrina and I sipped champagne at the foot of our sparkling baby Christmas tree and asked ourselves, "What the hell are we doing?"

Neither of us had a clue. We still had no real friends and the city felt more fragile and unsettled than ever. The threat of terrorism had intensified, our loneliness had increased, my finances were precarious at best, and neither of us had a plan for the future.

Looking out the window at the now very gray, very dark, very wounded, cold winter sky, eating a few roasted chestnuts we had purchased off a street vendor on the corner nearby, we asked each other if we thought we should stay.

We both fell silent and thoughtful, considering all that was going on both inside and out. After a very long moment, we lifted our glasses and toasted, saying, "Hell yes, we should." And that settled that.

Part Four

THE SANCTUARY

Third Apartment
Is a Charm

Having spent the last nine months in the Old Man, I began to realize that, as nice as the apartment was compared to the Old Lady, the fact was that it was a very expensive—and very noisy—furnished apartment, and if I really wanted to make Paris my home, we needed to move one more time.

Still, I was reluctant to move for one simple reason: I had learned to live without owning anything other than my clothing. I was deeply reluctant to begin to acquire stuff again. In not owning anything, I could easily pick up and go anytime I wanted to, and that was a freeing feeling.

On the other hand, I wanted to get grounded and belong in Paris, not just be a voyeur. After going back and forth over this for a few weeks, I finally decided at the end of January to begin the process of looking for a new, unfurnished apartment. It was time.

The hunt was on. I began my search by looking online at several real estate websites. There I saw some pretty hideous apartments, all without kitchens or lighting fixtures, which I thought was very bizarre.

When I asked about this, I was told that traditionally rental apartments in France come without these two basics, and that it is up to the renter to buy the appliances, cabinets, and light fixtures for the kitchen and then hire someone to install them. Moreover, one agent told me that when a tenant leaves, if he does not take his appliances and cabinets with him, the owner tears them out and discards them, even if everything is brand-new, leaving the new tenant to begin all over again from scratch.

This sounded so crazy I couldn't believe it. It was another quirk of living here I guess, but something I had absolutely no interest or confidence in getting involved with doing. It was complicated enough to arrange the most basic of things, like getting a bank account and cell phone.

The prospect of arranging to build a kitchen on my own, in France, in French, was simply inconceivable. I immediately began to pray to my angels and guides to help me find an apartment that had a kitchen already installed, and at a price I could afford. Believing in miracles, I kept searching.

One day I happened upon a new website that offered beautiful unfurnished apartments for rent throughout Paris. After looking at a few of the ones they featured, I became very encouraged. At least *some* of the apartments had kitchens, if not lighting fixtures.

I quickly made an inquiry and filled out the online questionnaire asking me what I was looking for in great detail, then I crossed my fingers. Two days later I received an e-mail from a gentleman in the real estate office who told me he had several options to show me that would meet my criteria in the 16th *quartier,* if that neighborhood interested me.

This was an area of Paris I was not familiar with at all, but I was open. In my mind, Paris is small, and all of it, or at least most of it, is interesting to me. Besides, between walking and the métro, it was easy to get to just about anywhere I wanted to in less than 30 minutes, so the neighborhood didn't matter that much if the apartment was nice.

I eagerly agreed to meet him the following day at noon at the address he gave me, near the place Victor Hugo, where he said he would show me three available apartments, all near one another.

I arrived early and walked around, exploring the neighborhood a bit. There were some lovely restaurants and cafés surrounding a beautiful fountain in the middle of the plaza. Across from the plaza were a greengrocer, an artisanal bakery, a large pharmacy, some little clothing shops, and an ice cream shop, all of which made the area appealing.

Wandering back to the address I was given, I waited for another 15 minutes before my agent showed up, now 20 minutes late. To my surprise, he literally roared up on the sidewalk. There he was, all of five feet tall at most, dressed in a puffy black leather jacket, black leather pants, and black motorcycle boots. He sported a huge black, bulbous motorcycle helmet and sat on top of a humongous Harley-Davidson, reminding me an awful lot of the cartoon character Atom Ant.

Snapping the engine off and tossing a cigarette to the ground as he descended the beast of a bike, he then slipped off the black globe helmet to reveal a surprisingly small head to go with his surprisingly small body.

"Are *you* Monsieur Thomas?" I asked in French as he walked toward me, just to be sure. I had expected to be met by a reserved older gentleman in a beige coat with a beige scarf around his neck, in typical conservative French style, instead of this Lilliputian version of an upscale Hell's Angel.

"Oui, tout à fait, Madame Choquette," he answered, and then switched to English, which I noticed many French people did when I spoke to them in French. "Shall we go in?"

He then turned toward the building we were standing in front of and quickly pushed a code on a huge double door, which let us into a magnificent gray stone and marble courtyard. Once inside, we were met by an exceedingly handsome and elegantly dressed concierge, who greeted us as if we were celebrities walking into a five-star hotel. This was an entirely different side of Paris from the one I knew, and one that I liked very much.

I was so fascinated by all that was unfolding before me that I unfortunately wasn't watching where I was going. As Monsieur Thomas motioned for us to walk into a second entryway on the right, I failed to see that there was a small step in front of me, which I promptly tripped over, falling flat on my face, both hands still in my coat pockets. Talk about being ungrounded.

Looking up, mortified, I could see both Monsieur Thomas and the doorman were just as mortified looking down at me. I rebounded like an Olympic gymnast and was back on both feet in two seconds flat.

Monsieur Thomas didn't ask if I was okay, as he was so shocked to see me down and back up so fast, all without the use of my hands, but I nevertheless assured both him and the doorman that I was "just fine."

Grateful that Monsieur Thomas said nothing, I followed him toward the slightly larger than normal, but still sardine can–sized, French elevator and entered. He pushed the button for the third floor.

I thought the building where I lived was nice, but this was an entirely new level of luxury all the way around, and I was really excited to see what was in store. Monsieur Thomas was silent as we rode up, facing straight ahead. Once we arrived, he simply opened the door and let me in, then stepped aside, still not saying a word.

The apartment was jaw-droppingly stunning. It had high ceilings and wall-to-wall, floor-to-ceiling windows that opened up onto a private courtyard below, with gorgeous dark wood parquet floors—unusual for Paris. The apartment itself was very large, with four bedrooms, all completely renovated to the highest standard. It had a large freestanding soaking tub; a huge, state-of-the-art eat-in kitchen; and walls and walls and *walls* of—unheard of—built-in cedar closet space. Everything in the apartment, from the cabinets to the bathroom fixtures to the closets and more, was the top of the line in quality.

It was spectacular. I was ready to take it on sight and said so. Having shared my rent limit online, I couldn't believe that I was being shown this apartment, but hey, who was I to question? Expecting the rent to be in the range of the limit I had stated, I nearly gagged when Monsieur Thomas told me that it was in fact 11,000 euros a month.

"Monsieur Thomas," I said, flabbergasted, "why on earth are you even showing this apartment to me? The rent is over four times higher than I said I wanted to spend. I should have never been shown this. I cannot afford it, and now everything I see from here on out will look terrible in comparison."

He shook his head and agreed with me, absolutely ignoring my question.

"Yes, you are right. Everything from here on out will most likely look worse than terrible," he answered unapologetically.

"Aw, come on, Monsieur Thomas. No fair. I was so excited looking around, as this is the best apartment I have ever seen."

"I am certain it is one of the best apartments you will *ever* see," he answered. "Are you sure you do not want to take it?" he continued, completely ignoring the fact that I just said I could not afford it.

"I *do* want to take it, Monsieur Thomas. But I cannot afford it. So we might as well leave right now.

"Monsieur Thomas," I asked as he locked the door behind us and headed back toward the elevator, "did you receive my criteria for the apartment and what I was looking for?"

"Yes," he said.

"And the price I was willing to spend?"

"Yes," he said.

"Yet, this was so much more."

"Yes," he said.

"Is it normal to show people something they cannot afford?"

"What people can afford and what they suggest they are willing to spend are often very different. I prefer to show you this apartment, just in case."

"Well, in my case, Monsieur Thomas," I replied, "what I said that I wanted to spend and what I *can* spend are pretty much the same, just so you know. So no more torture, okay?"

"Okay," he answered. *"Pas de problem. On y va."*

And with that we took the elevator down and left the building, saying a final *au revoir* to the doorman. Once outside we turned and walked to a building a few doors south to see the second of the three apartments he had in mind.

This building also needed a door code to enter, but once inside, there was no gorgeous entryway or handsome doorman to greet us as before. Instead we found ourselves inside a dark, stinky entryway. Monsieur Thomas rang the *gardien's* bell on a door just inside and to the right, and an angry woman answered, fiercely complaining that it was lunchtime and how dare he disturb her before 1:30 P.M.

Standing back, not wanting to catch her ire, Monsieur Thomas apologized profusely and asked for the key to the apartment so he could show it to me. While he did that I glanced around at the shabby surroundings. It wasn't easy because the lightbulb in the light fixture above us was burned out, making it difficult to see much in the dark.

Key in hand, we found our way to a small elevator and got in and headed to the fourth floor. Once we stepped outside we were face-to-face with the apartment's front door. Monsieur Thomas jiggled the key for a few seconds and then swung open the door, letting us into the dreariest, dirtiest apartment I had seen yet.

The walls were nearly black, although originally beige in color, with large chunks of plaster falling off of them and all over the floor. There was no kitchen this time, and the rooms were quite small and chopped up. This apartment made the Old Lady look like the Ritz.

I took two steps in and stopped. "Monsieur Thomas, this is awful. It will never do."

"Of course," he said, and turned on his heels, following me as we left. We were in and out of the building in less than five minutes, the *gardien* yelling after us not to disturb her ever again during the lunch hour.

Once outside, I looked at Monsieur Thomas and asked, "Is it going to be this bad from here on out?"

He nodded his head and said, "Perhaps. Are you sure you do not want to take the other apartment?"

I nodded mine back and said, "Yes."

He then told me to meet him in 15 minutes at the third apartment, about a half mile from where we were, pointing to a taxi stand on the plaza. Then he popped his huge helmet back on his head and jumped on his motorcycle, as if he were Clint Eastwood jumping on a black stallion, and roared off.

I strolled over to the taxi stand and got in a taxi, in no rush to get to the next address, as I had a sinking feeling that it, too, would be a grand disappointment. It was.

The building was as shabby as the last, and there was not even a *gardien* this time, which was also a bad sign. There was also no elevator, so we walked up the five flights of stairs to the apartment.

When he opened the door, we were flooded with light, and for a split second I thought *maybe* this apartment would be okay. In fact, it was huge. There were four bedrooms and a double salon, but the floor plan was all chopped up and felt very disjointed.

Once again there was neither a kitchen nor lighting fixtures, and the one bathroom was ancient and filthy. After looking around for a minute, I said, "Sorry, Monsieur Thomas, this place is not for me."

He knew before I said anything. Once we were on the sidewalk outside of the building, standing once again in front of his giant motorcycle, I said, "The truth is, Monsieur Thomas, I want a smaller version of the first apartment. I want it to be as clean and as nicely painted, *with* a kitchen, and with positive energy just like the other one, and at my price. I know it's out there somewhere. I feel it. You just have to find it."

He shook his head. "It is doubtful," he answered.

Not to be deterred, as the French tend to be pessimistic by nature, I continued. "Maybe so. But I am an optimistic American and a believer in miracles."

He raised his eyebrow at that statement and looked as though I might be crazy. I ignored this and continued.

"And if anyone can find this place, Monsieur Thomas, I am sure it will be you. In the meantime, I'll be patient and wait for it to show up."

Again he raised his eyebrow and said, "Doubtful, but we will see."

Then I said, "Now I will go home and nurse my hip and sore shins. They are hurting from the fall." He winced and said, "I am not surprised. You fell pretty hard."

I just laughed.

We shook hands on that, then he popped his helmet on once again and revved the engine on his bike super loud. He roared off, disappearing into the winter mist hanging over the city.

I limped along avenue Raymond Poincaré to place Victor Hugo, continued on to the Champs-Elysées, over avenue Montaigne to Pont de l'Alma, across the Seine, and then up avenue Bourdonnais, wondering all the way if he would find me an apartment. My lease wasn't up for another three and a half months, so I had time on my side.

On the way home I walked into a shop called Agnes and looked around, trying to get grounded and settle my mind. There I found a white shirt on a hanger, begging to be tried on.

"Oh, you again," I said under my breath, taking it in my hand. "Do you think I'm ready now for a white shirt and my own real French apartment?"

I tried it on and found it fit. "I guess this means yes to both questions," I said to myself, buying it on the spot. "I hope so anyway," I continued as I put it and the receipt in my bag. "At the moment neither you nor the apartment feels entirely comfortable to me, but I'm going to go for it anyway."

By the time I got back to the Old Man, however, I wondered if I was making a mistake. It would be so much easier in so many ways just to stay put. Yet, I knew in my heart that a need for a real home—and lower rent—was beckoning me onward. We were moving. I just didn't know where.

Avenue M!

Traveling back and forth to the U.S. and Mexico for work allowed both Sabrina and me to escape the terminal winter gray of Paris over the next month. We even managed to spend a week in Costa Rica with Sonia and some old friends. I was at first surprised at how many French people were there along with us. But knowing how dreary Paris is at this time of year, it made perfect sense.

The apartment search dragged on. I looked at two or three apartments a week when I was back in Paris, all more or less as sad as the ones before. Then one day I received a note from Monsieur Thomas saying he found exactly what I was looking for and suggested we rendezvous as soon as possible before the apartment was leased to someone else.

Excited to hear this news, and noticing the address was not far from the Arc de Triomphe, I beelined over the next day, this time with Sabrina alongside, to see if it could possibly be true.

As we approached the building, I could see Monsieur Thomas in the distance, leaning against his massive bike, helmet in hand, smoking a cigarette, waiting for us. I told Sabrina he was our agent, and she said, "You're kidding. The little guy all decked out in leather?"

"Yes, that's him. He's rocking his style, Bean. Got to give him credit for that," I answered.

"You're right, Mom. He most certainly *is* rocking his look."

The street itself, on the other hand, was not nearly as colorful as Monsieur Thomas. In fact, it was mostly made up of office buildings with only a few cafés. The Champs-Elysées was 200 feet away, however, and with that, the main métro line to everywhere.

Upon arrival we shook hands with Monsieur Thomas and turned to enter the building, this one without a code. After he pushed the entry button, the door opened up into a beautiful foyer. To the left was a grand staircase, with an almost normal-size elevator at the foot of it. It was all very impressive.

Monsieur Thomas said the apartment he would be showing us was on the second floor, so Sabrina and I elected to walk up while he took the elevator. When we arrived, we saw that there was only one huge double door on the floor. Monsieur Thomas unlocked it and led us into another, smaller foyer opening onto two apartments, one to the left and one to the right.

He unlocked the door to the right and revealed a gorgeous entryway leading into a place so newly refurbished that it still had the smell of fresh paint. The apartment had higher ceilings than even the luxurious one Monsieur Thomas had first shown me on avenue Victor Hugo, allowing light to flood in and giving it the appearance of being even bigger than it was, and it wasn't small to begin with. It had typical floor-to-ceiling French doors; two large bedrooms; a den; a simple but very workable kitchen equipped with brand-new appliances, their price tags still on them; and two brand-new bathrooms, one complete with a bath tub. It also had a washer and dryer (for what that was worth) and huge floor-to-ceiling built-in closets in both bedrooms.

Outside the French doors there was a balcony that ran along the entire length of the apartment, where we could sit or stand, and if we stretched far enough out, we could actually see the Arc de Triomphe.

Monsieur Thomas told us that in any building designed during the 19th-century renovation of Paris by Baron Haussmann (which this had been), the second-floor apartments had the highest ceilings and a balcony, because they were built for the nobles of the time.

When I opened the doors to the balcony onto the street below, it was somewhat noisy, with four lanes of traffic, but when I shut them, the noise was completely silenced. Monsieur Thomas reassured us that the traffic became much slower and quieter at night, and the noise would not be a problem. Even with the traffic below and the less-than-exciting neighborhood, it was a fantastic apartment and just the miracle I had prayed for.

I looked suspiciously at Monsieur Thomas. "Is this something we can *afford?"*

"Yes," he replied. "In fact, it is five hundred euros less than your limit, which I cannot believe. Really it's incredible. You must take it, as I have never seen something like this at this price."

I asked what the catch was, as clearly something this nice had potential drawbacks of which I was unaware at the moment.

"Honestly, I am puzzled over this rental price, as this apartment clearly commands more rent than the owner is asking for. But never question when the price is too low. Only when it is too high," he answered.

He then told us that almost everyone in the building, except for the *gardien,* went home at 6 P.M., as they were business tenants, so we would be the only ones left at night. "It will be very quiet, and you can even have a very loud party if you want to," he suggested. The promise of this level of quiet was enormously appealing given the constant barrage of noise we were exposed to on a daily basis living in our present apartment. It just kept getting better and better.

I asked about the neighbors across the hall in the other apartment. He said the apartment belonged to a young Romanian couple with a six-year-old daughter, and they normally lived in Bucharest. They came every once in a while to Paris, but not too often. This was their French *atelier.* The fact that they were Romanian sealed the deal. At least if they ever heard me and Sabrina arguing loudly with each other behind our door, they would totally understand, so we wouldn't have to be too self-conscious.

He also said the *gardiens* of the building were third generation and very kind and welcoming. That was comforting, as our present *gardien* was hardly that. In fact, on our way out, Monsieur Thomas rang the bell and introduced us to the *gardien,* Madame

Tottet. She said to call her Céline and that she and her husband, David, would be delighted to have us as tenants in the building, all of which made the apartment seem even more like it could be a happy home. As soon as we said good-bye and walked out, Monsieur Thomas asked if I would be taking the apartment. I said, "Yes, absolutely."

"Good decision," he answered. "You are very lucky with such a good place."

"I knew you would find it, Monsieur Thomas. My intuition told me so. Well done and thank you very much. I am grateful."

We shook hands and he said he would get the paperwork started immediately. He then popped his bulbous black helmet back on his head and roared off on his black stallion of a bike, and we turned to walk back toward our apartment.

As we walked home, Sabrina immediately turned to me and said, "See, Mom? The miracles just keep coming. This apartment is perfect for us. It's so beautiful and so bright and sunny and quiet and new and clean and affordable and *everything* we asked for. I think we will love it."

"I do too, Sabrina," I answered. "After all the lousy apartments we've looked at over the past few months, I cannot believe we were shown something so fabulous."

We walked around the neighborhood for a few minutes to get a better sense of it but had to get back for work, so couldn't go far. We decided we would come back and look around later that evening. On the way back to the apartment, we passed a church and spontaneously decided to quickly dive in and light a candle in gratitude for our miracle. It was important.

"Thank you, angels. Thank you, God," I prayed quietly as I lit the largest candle they had, putting 10 euros in the offering box for it. "Just when I think I am at a dead end, you keep opening things up and surprising me with such beautiful blessings. I am so grateful. It reminds me to keep expecting good things, even if I don't know where they will be coming from." And with a hearty "Amen," I turned to Sabrina and we nodded to each other to leave.

Then we nearly ran back home so we wouldn't be late for work.

On the way home a whole new wave of concerns began to hit me, mostly because Monsieur Thomas had said the minimum lease the owners offered was for three years. That was a lot more of an emotional commitment than one year. I asked Sabrina again if she thought it was the right decision.

"Mom, where else would you want to go?" Sabrina asked. "We have no ties in Chicago, save for Sonia, and she visits us all the time. It is so exciting to live here, in spite of the challenges, so I say we go for it all the way."

She was right. I had been in fight-or-flight mode ever since the divorce, and it was time to stop the flight and settle down. And truthfully, as romantic as it seemed to be able to just get up and go, having no real sense of home created anxiety. While the two apartments we had been living in over the past year were interesting and colorful, they were temporary and, underneath it all, not ours to call home.

If the outside mirrored the inside, this brand-new "miracle" apartment implied positive things to come. It was calm in the new building, which promised an internal calm that I desperately needed now. In the end I knew it was a gift and we needed to jump in headfirst and take it.

On Strike

Saying good-bye to Jean Luc was difficult, as he had been a great landlord and friend over the past year. We were sad to leave and told him so. Jean Luc would have none of this sentimentality, insisting we would remain friends despite our leaving and would see each other again in no time. He understood our need to get a more substantial home at a better price and was enthusiastic we had found something that worked for us and was so nearby.

Packing up and moving again wasn't easy. It was amazing how much more we had accumulated since we arrived a year ago, and we didn't have enough suitcases to transport it all. To solve the problem, we decided to move over several days, loading up the suitcases, taking things to the new apartment in quick taxi rides, unloading them, and then returning with empty suitcase to do it all over again. This plan, though tedious, worked out well. By the end of the second day, with the last suitcases stuffed into the trunk of the final waiting taxi, and with a flurry of French double-cheek air kisses for Jean Luc, Alice, and Alex, we were out of Belgrade and on our way to our new home.

Once arrived, we realized that we now had to get busy with the task of making this blank slate of an apartment into a home. It seemed cavernous when we finally closed the door behind us and looked at our mountain of stuff piled in the middle of the living room floor.

"Here we are Sabrina," I said, my voice echoing under the 14-foot ceilings with no furniture to absorb the sound. Daunted by the reality that we would now have to get *everything* we needed, from silverware to pots and pans to rugs and more, I added, "I hope we made the right decision."

Just then Sabrina looked out the window to the avenue below us and shouted, "Mom, look outside. There are hundreds of beautiful horses lined up on the street with military guards standing next to them!"

Sure enough, right outside our window, as if they had appeared out of nowhere, were what seemed like a thousand or more military horses lined up according to color, with white to tan horses in the front, graduating to caramel-colored ones, and then to black horses in the back, their guards standing next to them wearing beautiful uniforms, including helmets with long horse tails flowing from the top.

I don't how they arrived so fast, as we had been in the apartment for only about 20 minutes.

"Looks like Paris sent the Royal Guard to welcome us here, Mom," said Sabrina, looking up on her iPhone who and what they might be, having never seen such a magnificent sight here in Paris—or pretty much anywhere—before.

"Oh my God! You're right," I said, laughing at the impressive sight below us, the horses huge and magnificent, the guards standing at attention at their side. We opened the balcony doors and stepped outside and into the drizzle to get a better look, feeling lucky to have such an unobstructed bird's-eye view of the entire regiment (which ran for about a mile) from the second floor where we were perched.

"What a great way to begin our life here. Thank you, angels, for such a fabulous welcome!" I shouted out on the street.

Apparently they could hear me shout from below, as there was no traffic, because several of the guards looked up at us and smiled, breaking from formation now and starting to brush and groom their horses, while people gathered around and took photos.

The arrival of the Garde républicaine, as the military horse guards were called, banished the creeping anxiety I was just starting to feel about having to furnish the place. Because of this unexpected greeting committee, I relaxed, knowing in my heart that it would all work out.

Moments later, the Garde républicaine began mounting their horses and started to move on toward the Arc de Triomphe at the end of the avenue, as though their mission to escort and welcome us had now been accomplished.

We stepped back inside and out of the rain and high-fived each other. "Let yet another adventure in Paris begin," I said to Sabrina, opening the tiny bottle of champagne we had set aside for this occasion. We sipped from the tiny plastic cups that came with it, as we had no glasses.

"I can toast to that," she said, enjoying the moment. "You never know what is going to happen next around here. I love it!"

After several visits to the glorious home-furnishing emporium BHV in the Marais and one infuriating trip to IKEA in the suburbs, the only things we were waiting on to make our apartment complete were two sofas. We had ordered them almost immediately after we found the apartment, but were told we would have to wait eight weeks for delivery, as they came from Belgium.

Then all hell broke loose in Paris, as we faced one strike after the other for the entire month of April. There was a transportation strike, a student strike, a garbage strike, a gasoline strike, an air traffic controller strike, a nurses' strike, and who knows what other strike, because we didn't follow the news. We just realized that chaos was unfolding everywhere because of the relentless demonstrations in the streets.

At first the strikes didn't create problems for us, so we merrily continued to mind our own business and hoped that calm would return for the Parisians soon. Then I received a call that our awaited sofas would not be delivered as promised because the transportation strike and the gasoline strike prevented deliveries from coming in from Belgium.

When I asked how soon before they would arrive, the woman from the shop said my guess was as good as hers. She tried to be reassuring in a French way, saying perhaps it would only be a matter of weeks if we were lucky, but then she backed out of her optimism, emphasizing, once again, a very skeptical *if we were lucky.*

Hanging up, I delivered the bad news to Sabrina. We agreed not to let this annoy us and positioned one of the mattresses on the living room floor, saying this would be our sofa for now. Knowing it was futile to be upset, we decided to go with the flow and save our peace of mind. In the meantime we would simply continue to make our apartment feel like a home in other ways. We set up our kitchen and bathrooms. We organized our closets, and then we went in search of lights.

Looking for lighting fixtures took us to antique fairs and flea markets around Paris that we, surprisingly, hadn't yet visited the entire time we'd been there. It was a world unto itself—miles of gloriously cool things to buy, from antique paintings to mirrors to candlesticks to lace tablecloths to great pieces of old furniture to quirky coatracks, all of which left me wishing I had considered looking here for stuff for our home before going to IKEA.

Our greatest finds were two fantastic antique cut-glass chandeliers that I immediately knew would look gorgeous hanging from our high ceilings. I told the seller I loved them but was hesitant to buy, as I had no one to help me properly hang them up.

He assured me that this was not a problem and said he would arrange for his handyman to come and install them the very next day. That was all I needed. Impulsive as I am, I bought them on the spot. We shook hands and he said he would be at the apartment at 9 A.M.

The very next day the antiques dealer showed up, on time, with the disassembled chandeliers in boxes, the handyman right behind him, tools and a ladder in tow. Behind him was the man's wife, there to help.

The minute she walked in and saw me, she gasped. Worried that she was sick, I immediately asked her if she was all right and invited her to sit on the floor mattress. She nearly burst into tears and said she knew who I was, had read all of my books for years and years, and that I had changed her life. It was surprising, as I am not usually randomly recognized for my work in France and had only had the experience a few times, once at the Apple store and once at the famous English-language bookstore, Shakespeare and Company. She then told her husband that he had to do the very best job and give me a big discount for the installation as she had been so helped by me. I took this as another sign that we were definitely on the right path.

A few hours later the lights were installed. They lit up the apartment beautifully. One chandelier had little stars etched into the glass, of which I had been unaware, and they cast beautiful little star shadows across the walls when the light was on. I felt the angels all around us with this starry surprise and was so grateful for their uplifting presence.

On the way out the door, Amélie, the wife, said that she and her husband, Christophe, were available any time should we ever need handiwork and gave us her card. They would be right over, she assured me. Knowing we would have such practical help if we needed it was greatly reassuring and yet another sign that we were moving in the right direction.

The new apartment was wonderful, and even though we had no sofas, we nevertheless felt incredibly at home. The overall natural stress and underlying anxiety of moving for the third time now subsiding, both Sabrina and I were taken by how calm we felt in this new space. The building was absolutely quiet at night as promised. It had been so long since I had felt that level of serenity, it took some getting used to. It was like living in a sensory-deprivation tank compared to the old place.

I finally received a phone call, after what turned out to be a four-week delay, that the sofas were to arrive at 8 A.M. a few days later. I was so excited to hear this news that I was up and dressed by 6 A.M. on delivery day. Eight o'clock came and went, then 9, and then 10. Finally, at 10:30, I called the shop and asked where the delivery guys were.

The shop called the truck and asked the driver to call me back directly. Several moments later, I received a call from the delivery man. He said he had been there at eight, but since there was no door code, he didn't know how to get in and left.

I said he just had to push the button, as the door wasn't locked, and to please come back. He then said he couldn't come back as he had other deliveries to make. When I asked when he would be coming back, he said it would be another four weeks.

"Four more weeks!" I cried. "No way! You are in Paris and the door is open! Just come back now." I even asked where he was. He was less than a mile away.

He said it was impossible.

I wanted to scream in frustration.

This made no sense, but I was beginning to learn that in France there was no arguing with these things. Having experienced this level of frustration several times since signing my lease and setting up my household, I knew the routine. I took a deep breath. Then 10. Then 20. *Then* I called the shop.

It would do no good to call and be upset. French service people generally don't take any responsibility for miscommunications like this, and if you dare to get angry or upset with them, they simply hang up on you if you are on the phone, or tell you they will not work with you if you are with them in person. In fact, there is a big sign at the Orange phone store, another infuriating place of business with which I had the pleasure of working when I had to get telephone and Internet installed in the new apartment, that says if you speak angrily toward any staff member *ever*, they will call the police and have you arrested. I am convinced to this day that the daily sport among the staff of every single Orange store in Paris is to see how many people they can first drive mad with their rude and dismissive treatment and then have the police come and arrest.

When I explained to the woman at the furniture store that the delivery men had come and gone and hadn't even *tried* to get into the building or call, even though I had told them the door was *not* locked *and* given them my phone number, all I received in reply was a disinterested, "I'm sorry someone dropped the ball on that."

When I asked what could be done, I was told nothing could be done. I simply had to wait until the next delivery cycle and *hopefully* it would work out then.

I gave up. I called upon the Serenity Prayer to help me, as I was really, *really* frustrated. "Lord, *please* help me accept the things I cannot change, and have the *intelligence* to remember I am in *France,* where I can change *nothing!*" It was mind-blowing, but I knew there was a lesson in all of this.

For one thing, I knew that as with any relationship, my relationship with my adopted country included both the good and the bad. So far, I had enjoyed a great romance with the "good" Paris. Clearly that phase was ending, and my relationship with the *real* Paris was now beginning. I had to accept the whole enchilada, so to speak, if I were to make my home here, including the bureaucracy, the one-way-street way of doing things, the refusal of anyone *ever* to take responsibility for a problem. The slowness. The disinterest and even disdain shown to customers in some places of business. And the powerlessness I felt over many things. I now had to accept it all.

"Okay, God," I said out loud as I took another breath. "I give up. I'm not going to control this, so I guess I'll have to control myself instead. I'm not going to have a fit. I'm going to be patient. I accept there is nothing I can do about the sofa situation, so I'll choose to be calm." Since I was up and dressed, I decided to go sit at a café and enjoy watching the world go by. The café au lait was pure perfection that morning. So was the delicious croissant I ordered along with it. And the apple tarte and mini baguette with jam. It was the perfect way to calm down.

Crash and Burn

It was inevitable. The moment I had put the last touches on the apartment, after spending a fortune and nearly losing my mind dealing with the French bureaucracy in order to make it happen, and was ready to finally settle into a real Paris home with Sabrina, she moved to London with friends.

While I struggled to put on a happy face when with her, and in my soul really *did* feel happy for her, at the same time I felt utterly and totally abandoned by her, which wasn't something I was especially proud of or wanted her to know. The truth was, however, that her move devastated me.

My partner in crime, my playmate, and my only friend in Paris had split just as soon as the ink was barely dry on my three-year lease, leaving me feeling completely trapped and alone.

I was shocked at how deeply upset and overwhelmed I was by her leaving. Especially since I was genuinely happy for her and knew in my heart and spirit that was absolutely what she must do. And besides, she left home six years earlier. It wasn't like I hadn't seen her go before.

But in the quiet moments between bouts of tears, it became more and more apparent that I wasn't just crying over Sabrina's departure. I was finally and fully grieving my divorce and the end of my life as I knew it. Until now, I had been more or less running and running, keeping the deepest of my feelings at bay ever since I came to Paris. Now, as I slowed down and Sabrina stepped away, I was faced with what I had been secretly running from: the death of my old life, as well as the fear of being all alone in this new one.

I almost laughed at the absurdity of my predicament. I chose to be here. I worked hard to stay. I gladly signed the lease. I spent a fortune to create my home. Now I was stuck. And as always, I had to surrender to the realization that this was exactly what my soul needed, even if I hated it. My worst fear was upon me. I was alone and had no one to ease my pain. Fuck!

I was acutely aware that there was a part of me watching, guiding, and reassuring me this was a necessary part of my soul's journey, and while I fully trusted this deeply intuitive part of me, this soul part of me, the emotional *human* part of me was freaking out.

I was in pain and was ashamed that I was in pain. I knew I was supposed to be here, in this beautiful and complicated city, in this state of aloneness, and at this time in my life, but that didn't make me feel one bit better. If anything, I was deeply disappointed that all my spiritual knowledge and prayers didn't protect or insulate me from my pain. Still, all I could do was pray, meditate, and pray some more. And be patient with my own transformational process.

To make matters worse, I got physically sick the day after Sabrina's announcement. *Really* sick. I came down with a strange strain of bronchitis that resisted even the best France's medical system had to offer. I had a fever of 102 on and off and languished in bed for the next six weeks, through the end of May and nearly the entire month of June, with absolutely no energy to speak of. It took every ounce of strength and determination in me to simply get out of bed and get something to eat. Some days I didn't even do that. I had no appetite or interest in food. I was completely stopped dead in my tracks. No more running. No more distractions. No more focusing on everything around me. No more anything. I just lay in bed with my fears, my grief, and my all-consuming loneliness. I *had* to make friends now or I wouldn't get better. I just knew it in my heart.

Growing up in a family of seven kids and marrying a man from a family of nine meant that I had rarely ever been alone my entire life. I never had my own room, my own clothes, even my own name growing up, as I was named after my mother. I was used to being in the middle of a crowd. Even my work as an intuitive guide deeply immersed me in other people's energy every single day. Being truly alone came as shock to my system.

My new soul assignment was to finally and fully become grounded in me—Sonia—in my spirit and my connection to the divine and to other human beings as a fellow soul. I needed to make friends who didn't need me to serve, assist, uplift, or intuitively direct them, as I had felt so many of those who were no longer part of my life had been, but rather who simply loved and enjoyed me because I was lovable and enjoyable. I needed friends who would see and accept me without projections and filters and would just want to enjoy life with me. I had to fully embody and believe they existed and that I would attract them.

Thankfully, after several weeks of misery, the bronchial funk that had gripped my lungs finally began to lift. Feeling physically a little better, I had a sudden impulse to resume yoga to get moving once again. I looked online and found a studio only three blocks away, so I booked a beginner class at noon.

My luck continued, as the yoga teacher was a sweet Japanese woman who taught an *easy* class. There were just three other people in the class along with me: two youngish French women and a middle-aged Brazilian man.

When I walked out of the studio and into the lobby after class, the Brazilian man followed me, asking if I wanted to try some of his special Brazilian honey and offered me a small bottle of it for free. He said it was a natural antiseptic and had powerful healing qualities unlike any other in the world. According to him, it was "magic." He was trying to introduce it to the Paris market, which was why he gave me a jar to try.

"It's amazing," he said. "You will see."

I was delighted to accept his surprise offering, realizing that angels must have gotten me up and out and to this very class in order to receive this special gift. He said to take a small spoonful of it at a time and to use it sparingly, as it was so potent. I went home and drank nearly the entire bottle.

Amazingly, as promised, the next day I woke up and actually felt a *lot* better. I had more energy and even an appetite. My mood hadn't lifted, but at least I didn't feel like I was dying. It was a sign. It was time to get back in the flow.

Energized, I decided to go for a short walk in the bois de Boulogne, a beautiful, expansive forest near the edge of Paris, within walking distance of my new apartment.

It felt so good to be in this dense, soothing, quiet forest and away from the concrete of the city, only 20 minutes from my front door. Eventually I came upon a serene lake with a few people in paddleboats in the distance and a dozen young swans swimming nearby. As I sat down at the lake's edge to rest, overlooking the expanse of beauty before me, it became crystal clear that there was nothing more to run from or to. I had just needed a long soul rest. And being sick had forced me to take it.

The Euro Cup

I started to enjoy the summer again, in spite of my lingering heavy-heart hangover, and soon resumed my daily walks along the Seine and around town, appreciating the summer fun that had taken hold of the city.

The big news was that Euro Cup Soccer Tournament had descended upon Paris and would be here for the next six weeks, and with it came the entire male population of Europe and beyond. I had never seen so many packs of joyful men and boys roaming around town in groups. They were on the sidewalks, in the métros, on the buses, in cars, and in every nook and cranny of the city, with flags from every nation waving on their hats, shirts, shoes, bus and car windows, and any other place they could plant them. It was a sight to behold and a good way to observe what makes men happy.

As I watched, I laughingly found myself singing the '80s disco song "It's Raining Men" by the Weather Girls to myself, especially when it *was* raining (which it seemed to be doing often) and there were massive swarms of men headed over to the stadium or to the Champ-de-Mars in front of the Eiffel Tower to watch the next big match, either live or on the outdoor screen.

I couldn't help but catch the Euro Cup spirit, even though until moving here the only soccer games I had watched were my daughters' at the park on Saturday mornings, when they were little. Now I found myself paying attention to which countries were playing games when and got genuinely excited on the days when

France was playing, and more so when they won. No matter who won, each day fans from the winning team descended upon the streets of Paris en masse after the match, driving up and down, honking their horns, waving their national flags, and screaming with joy as they celebrated their win. The sense of fun was contagious. Paris went especially insane when France won, which was happening a lot. The festive atmosphere sucked me in and lifted my mood somewhat over those six weeks.

Night after night, France also breathed a sigh of relief at yet another terror-free day, as the threat of terrorism was at its highest level because of the crowds, and everyone was told to be on full alert at all times. The government issued a free app for smartphones that would go off and alert you if a terrorist attack occurred and then tell you what to do. Everyone in Paris was constantly reminded to download it. It was hard not to feel the intensity of this threat underneath all the fun. Still, I couldn't help but love and admire how people marched out in droves in defiance of any potential attack. Life was going on for all of us.

The games ended with the final match between France and Portugal, and the country went wild in anticipation of this huge event. I tuned in to watch the game on TV the night it happened. It was a long and boring game, and in the end France lost. In contrast to the exuberance everyone had displayed every night for the past six weeks, the streets of Paris were absolutely silent. This loss was an awful blow to the French morale, and no one made any attempt to cheer up. I was happy for Portugal but felt really disappointed not to be celebrating with France that night. After all the attacks they had suffered that year, I was hoping a win at the Euro Cup finale would offset some of the national suffering. Still, it was just a game, and there was always next year. Not many French people felt the same.

Despite the loss, France breathed a deep sigh of relief after the Euro Cup successfully ended without any terrorist attacks to mar it. So did I. Now, it was on to the celebrations of July 14th, Bastille Day, the French equivalent of our 4th of July. When the girls were young, we made a point of being in France at this time of year and always celebrated Bastille Day with picnics at the Champ-de-Mars while watching the fireworks.

Knowing this, and how down I had been feeling since she moved, Sabrina traveled back from London to spend two days with me. We spent Bastille Day shopping for our picnic and planned to go to the park around nine or so to enjoy the fireworks, only we burned ourselves out walking all over town during the day, so when it was time to leave for the park, both of us were too tired to go.

We laughed about this, as we had made such a big fuss about being together and upholding our Bastille Day tradition. We decided that we would enjoy our picnic on the floor in the apartment and then watch the fireworks from our balcony afterward instead, which was possible if we really craned our necks. After all, it was being together that mattered most. At 11:30 P.M., when the last sparklers died down, we decided to call it a day and go to bed, the stunning fireworks show over the Eiffel Tower leaving only a haze in the sky.

Just as I got into bed, however, for some unknown reason, I decided to look at CNN on my cell phone. Normally I would never do this just before sleep, so I wasn't sure why I was doing it now.

When I opened it up, I was stunned to see a breaking news report about a massacre on the boardwalk in Nice that had occurred only moments earlier, as revelers and their families were on their way home from watching the fireworks display down there, just as they were still doing in Paris.

Apparently a crazed terrorist crashed a 19-ton truck through the traffic barriers and down the boardwalk of the Promenade des Anglais at high speed, slamming into hundreds of innocent people, killing 84 and injuring another 434 before being killed himself. It was pure bloody mayhem and impossible to comprehend. Only seconds earlier, Sabrina and I had been basking in the afterglow of the fireworks, as no doubt those on the boardwalk were doing at the time their lives came to a horrific end. What an ambush.

The barbarity of this assault took my breath away. I didn't know how to get my head around it. I was heartsick and appalled beyond words and just sat back in stunned silence, trying to absorb what I had just learned. Sabrina came running in moments later.

"Mom, there was another terrorist attack in France. A horrendous one," she said.

"I know, Bean," I answered. "I just saw it on the news."

We just hugged one another and cried, not yet fully comprehending what had just happened. It felt like some unbelievably crazy, confused nightmare. I was just beginning to relax and feel at ease here, and now this. All I could think to do was pray, "Dear God, help us all."

A few minutes later our cell phones began to ring with family and friends from the States calling to be reassured that we were alive. Once they heard our voices, we heard over and over again that we should leave France *now*. *Good luck with that idea,* I thought, knowing how hunkered down I was in my new apartment. Despite the way this summer was unfolding, I didn't want to run away. This was my home now, and this was my life, both the good and the bad. I accepted it all. I was here for a reason, grounded deep in my soul. I felt it in my heart. I was here to stay.

Groucho Marx and Me

One day, to take my mind off the misery all around me, I decided to explore the neighborhood a little more and went for a walk. A few blocks from my apartment I came across a small, inviting shop called the Atelier du Sourcil. It was a place where women could have their eyebrows shaped, and the pictures in the window were of such beautiful women, young and old, that I just had to stop. As I read the sign, a pretty young woman stepped outside and asked me if I would like to come in and have my eyebrows shaped today, as they were just opening and offering a special for today only. Surprised by her kind manner, and in need of *some* sort of nurturing and connection, I spontaneously agreed.

The next thing I knew I was flat on my back on her table, a huge bright light shining in my face and the woman glaring down at me like she was about to undertake major surgery. Off to the races she went on my brows, tweezing, plucking, brushing, and tweezing some more. Twenty minutes later, with a very self-satisfied, *"Eh bien . . . voilà!"* she held up a mirror and showed me the results.

My eyebrows were bright red and very straight and thin now. After only a second, she whisked away the mirror and said, in French, "I need to darken them a little now for the full effect. Is that okay with you?"

"Okay, I guess," I answered, not sure what she meant. The next thing I knew, I found myself being attacked by a small device *tac-tac-tac*king first one brow and then the other. All the while she reassured me that whatever she was doing was *"magnifique!"*

I was aghast at what was happening but didn't know how to stop it. By the time I summoned the wherewithal to actually say "stop," she had already finished one brow, so I just let her go ahead with the second, hoping that whatever was happening to my eyebrows looked far better than it *felt!*

Ten minutes later, the attack stopped and a now very enthusiastic Lucille (as I read on her name tag as she drilled away) beamed proudly at her finished product and declared, *"Parfait! Très française."*

I smiled when I heard that, despite feeling far less "nurtured" than I imagined I would when I spontaneously agreed to do this only 30 minutes earlier. I grabbed the mirror, optimistically expecting to look like a beautiful brunette version of Brigitte Bardot. I nearly choked in horror when instead I saw Groucho Marx looking back at me in my reflection.

"What did you do to me?" I gasped in French, shocked at the two dark, reddish-brown, caterpillar-looking blobs sitting above my eyes in the place of my eyebrows.

"Don't panic," she said, smiling calmly in a reassuring way. "I tattooed your eyebrows for definition. It's wonderful, no?"

"No! It's *not* wonderful. It's awful," I cried, dark flashbacks of the *Coupe Énergique* taking hold. *"Why* does this keep on happening to me?" I groaned to myself. I just wanted to feel better and look beautiful.

"Don't worry. I promise you. It is not permanent. It will lighten up a lot in the next five days and you will love it," Lucille insisted, still full of confidence. "It is the coolest look for Paris now. You will see."

Horrified at what I had just allowed to happen, but choosing to remain cool, I calmed a little and said, "Okay, Lucille. I didn't know Groucho Marx eyebrows were a 'thing' in Paris this year, but I'm stuck with them now." And then, "Are you absolutely *sure* they will lighten up?"

"Absolutely," she answered now in English, since I don't speak French well when in shock and had quit trying five minutes earlier. Lucille continued, "It's always a *leetle* strong the first time, but after you will love it forever. It is very French and very beautiful."

"Okay." I fake-smiled as I paid her. "How much do I owe you for this *leetle, très française* surprise?"

"One hundred euros," she answered.

I nearly gagged. "You are kidding."

"No, it's a special today. Normally it is one hundred fifty euros. You are lucky."

"Right," I said as I pulled out my credit card and handed it over, feeling far, far from that.

"Oh, and by the way, do not wash the eyebrows for twenty-four hours to keep them perfect. It takes this time to set the dye," Lucille added as I walked out the door in a daze. As soon as I was out of view, I ran the rest of the way home.

The minute I walked into my apartment, I ran to the mirror and stared at myself. I looked as if I had two thick brownish-red worms lying across my forehead.

"Shit," I cried. "When will I ever learn!"

Once *again*, I had surrendered my common sense and power to a complete stranger and allowed her to lead me down the path to fashion-victim hell.

Panicked, I called Sabrina on Facetime.

The minute she answered I blurted out, "Sabrina I accidentally had my eyebrows tattooed. I didn't mean to. It just happened."

"It just happened? How did something like that *just happen*, Mom?" she answered in shock.

"I went into a beautiful shop to get my eyebrows shaped and the girl suggested I needed to darken them up, assuring me they would look beautiful, and the next thing I knew I left looking like Groucho Marx. That's how."

Staying calm, but clearly as alarmed as I was (I could tell by the look on her face), she said, "They're not so bad, Mom. They're a little *intense,* but not awful. Can you wash out the dye?"

Right! Wash it out. Lucille said not to touch them for 24 hours to let them set. If I washed them now, the dye wouldn't set.

"I'll call you back, Bean. I'm going to try that."

I then jumped up and ran to the bathroom, got some toothpaste and my nailbrush, and started to scrub and scrub my brows. It hurt like hell because that stupid tattoo gun had poked all these tiny little holes into them, but I ignored the burn. This was serious. I worked on scrubbing for 10 full minutes, continuing to add more and more tooth-whitening toothpaste every few seconds for good measure. To my utter relief, this actually lightened them a lot. Not completely, but enough to not cause me to flip out like I did with my *Coupe Énergique.* My eyebrows, now brilliant red from all the tweezing and plucking and tattooing and scrubbing with toothpaste, made me look like a rock lobster.

By then Sabrina was Facetiming me back. I answered and she asked, "Did that work? Let me see."

I walked to the light in the front room near the windows and stared at the screen so she could have a close look.

After studying me for a minute, she said, "They're much better now."

"You think?" I asked, needing her to say it again. Like 10 more times again.

"Yes, they're *much* lighter now," she reassured me. "They're still a little dark, but not as bad as before, thank God. You are lucky." That was the second time I'd heard that today. She then said, "Don't ever do that again, Mom. I mean it!"

"Are you kidding? I won't," I cried. "I didn't mean to do it the first time. The session just got away from me. I was feeling bad and just wanted a little uplifting care, that's all. I trusted she would take care of me."

"Next time get a massage, Mom, and don't ever go back in that shop."

"I will," I assured her. "I mean, I won't. I mean, I need to lie down now. I'm wiped out over this."

Sabrina signed off, telling me it was going to be okay, and I felt as if she were the mom and I was the kid. It was so embarrassing.

I looked up from the phone and saw my second stupid white shirt sitting on the dresser where it had been sitting for a while since I *never* wore it. I got up and threw it in the garbage. "Fuck looking chic and French!" I screamed at no one.

I went to bed and closed the door behind me. This was all just too damn much for me today. I needed a break.

Lying there in bed, I knew this was so ridiculous. Of course new eyebrows wouldn't make me feel better. But then again, yes they would. *I'm still a woman and it's okay to want a little pampering, and I like nice eyebrows,* I rationalized. *I just need to remember to stay in charge and in control of my experiences here in Paris. I'll get this right sooner or later,* I promised myself. *I just need to stop being so trusting and so damn naive. It definitely works against me.*

"I get it, Universe," I snapped out loud.

I know this is bigger than eyebrows. It's a lesson in taking charge of my self-care and self-love and not leaving it to others. The outside just mirrors the inside. Please, Universe, stop me if I am ever at risk of having this happen again.

"So French" my eye, I thought as I drifted off to sleep. *I'm done trying to be "tres Française." I just want to feel good as me.*

Phoenix Rising

It was now August and time for the annual Paris summer *vacances* again. This year I felt an overwhelming intuitive urge to go to Malta, a place I knew nothing about. I invited my daughters to join me, hoping this would uplift my spirits.

Sabrina met me in Paris and we traveled together, arriving at Malta's international airport a day before Sonia was to arrive from Chicago. When we got off the plane, I was surprised to see that the airport was absolutely packed, which I hadn't expected. In my mind Malta seemed so remote and, well, quiet. We quickly came to learn instead that it was one of the most popular summer destinations in Europe, as was obvious by the thousands of people swarming around us as we waited at baggage claim.

Once we grabbed our bags we took a taxi to the Airbnb we had rented, near St. Julian's Bay, which, according to our driver, was "the" area to be in. The winding roads leading into town were jam-packed with bumper-to-bumper cars, which only further dissipated all thoughts of a tranquil and restorative vacation.

The sensory assault continued once we entered the apartment, finding to our dismay that it was not at all the lovely place we had seen on the site, but rather a filthy dump. It looked as though a family of wild orangutans had vacated the place only moments earlier, leaving every sort of trash imaginable, including dirty diapers, and food on the floor. The mess was overwhelming. The maid, who apparently had arrived only moments before we did to clean up, also seemed to think so, as she wore a grossed-out expression.

We stood around for about 10 minutes in a confused "What do we do now?" state, then decided we couldn't stay. It would be impossible to relax here. We called the owner and said we were leaving and did. We took our bags with us and walked over to the seaside a few blocks away in search of a restaurant where we could eat lunch and figure out what to do next. I wished I had put more thought into the planning of this vacation, but I rarely do. I usually just show up and wing it, and for the most part this has served me well over the years.

I wasn't thrown off by this hiccup, however, and reassured Sabrina that we would sort this out and course correct by the time lunch was over.

I got online on my phone and searched for a hotel over lunch. They were all booked. Finally I found an Intercontinental Hotel not far from where we were that had a vacant room. We paid for lunch, grabbed a taxi, and made our way over to the hotel.

The hotel was only three kilometers from where we were and yet it took almost 30 minutes to get there due to the traffic. We could have walked there faster.

When we arrived, the area was so built up and dense, packed with sky-high strip clubs, bars, and malls, that it felt as though we were in Tokyo. St. Julian's Bay was a party town and not the blue lagoon I had envisioned in my mind.

"Where the hell are we?" Sabrina asked, confused by the scene. "This place is so strange!"

"I have no idea, Bean," I answered. "But I guess we will find out."

The hotel was beautiful and the most polite, attractive, tall young gentleman showed us to our room. While the room was small and nice enough, there was massive construction going on *directly* outside our window, on the 20th floor, complete with cranes and jackhammers and scrambling workers who looked inside our window and waved.

"No wonder they had a room," I said. "Too bad they didn't let us know we would be sharing it with a dozen voyeuristic construction workers."

We pulled the curtain closed and sat in the dark, wondering what to do. We decided to rally and check out the area. We would regroup again after Sonia arrived the next morning. I was determined to make this vacation work, although I wasn't sure how, because I hated it so far.

In spite of the crowds, the Maltese people were lovely, and everywhere we went the hospitality was warm and friendly. We walked around St. Julian's Bay and were entertained by the scene, as the beach was filled with thousands of young studs, gay and straight alike, flexing their muscles and cruising like packs of wild animals. It felt as if I had wandered into the wrong movie theater but was entranced by the show nevertheless.

We found a beautiful restaurant right on the bay and enjoyed a sunset dinner. Sabrina and I ordered champagne and toasted this strange adventure. Dinner was fabulous, and we both felt better. Yet still, there was an underlying heaviness for me here, and I didn't fully understand why.

Sonia showed up around noon the next day, as shocked and confused as we had been. "What is this place?" she asked. "It's feels like we could be in Times Square in New York. It doesn't even feel like Europe."

We agreed and decided that after she grabbed a nap, we would move to another area. We did some quick research and decided to go to the capital, Valletta, a few kilometers away. It looked much calmer and far more old-world and European.

We found a hotel online in Valletta, but got no answer when we called. Taking the bull by the horns and following my intuition I said, "Screw this. I'm going directly to the hotel to see if they have a room for us."

"I'll go with you," Sonia offered. Sabrina decided to stay and lie by the pool.

When we arrived at the hotel, the man at the front desk was very warm but apologized that there were no rooms available, as it was high season in Malta and every room on the island was booked. Not to be deterred, I asked him to ask the manager for a room for us, to which he seemed surprised but agreed. Moments later the manager stepped out and asked how he could help. I explained that our vacation was about to be ruined, as St. Julian's Bay was just not for us, and wondered if he might *please* find a room for us in this much calmer, more beautiful location.

Fully understanding, he took pity on us and started searching the computer. Five minutes later, he said that he could offer us a room beginning the next day and asked if we wanted to see it. The hotel was massive, but when we saw the room itself, it was perfect. The vacation was saved and we moved the next morning.

Valletta was a fascinating place; I had never been anywhere like it in all of my travels. Huge colorful religious flags flew throughout the picturesque small town overlooking the sea, evidently in preparation for a religious festival of some sort coming soon.

We learned from the concierge at the hotel later that afternoon that each town had its own patron saint, and these festivals were a part of their local identity and happened almost daily. In fact, the villages competed with each other over their saints' celebrations, with parades, fireworks displays, and live music. It was an elaborate and serious business around here, and everyone in each town got involved.

As charming as Valletta was, being here intensified the troubled feeling in me. I had so hoped to escape this heavy feeling when on vacation, but instead it got worse. It came to a head when we entered the St. John's Co-Cathedral and Museum in the center of Valletta the day after we arrived. An incredible Baroque masterpiece, it was built between 1573 and 1578 as a place of worship for the medieval Knights of St. John, closely associated with the Knights Templar.

This depressing feeling surprised me, as I've always had a deep soul connection to the Knights Templar and even wrote about this in my book *Walking Home*. I believe I was a Knight Templar myself in a past life and guarded the pilgrims on the Camino de Santiago. It's something I have vaguely felt for most of my life and have even dreamed of. I was never quite sure what I was dreaming, but it became crystal clear when I walked the Camino the first time. Now here I was in this cathedral where the Knights Templar were venerated perhaps more than anywhere in the world. There were more than 405 of these medieval knights' tombs under the polychrome marble floor in the center of the cathedral, with carved angels and skeletons dancing all over them.

As artistically impressive as this all was (indeed, it is one of the most beautiful Baroque churches in the world), the heaviness inside the cathedral nearly choked me. Yes, it was breathtakingly beautiful, but it was also a monument to patriarchy and war and death. I could only stay inside for about 15 minutes, listening to the audio guide, and then absolutely *had* to get out.

Once outside, I took a deep breath of fresh air. Feeling relieved, I walked over to a bench and sat down and waited for the girls, who were right behind me. Still, the negative energy followed me like a dark, heavy cloud. I tried to shake it off.

The town was busy preparing a massive celebration for St. Dominic, its patron saint, and even more huge colorful flags were being hung along the main grand pedestrian promenade as well as all along the side streets in preparation for the big parade tomorrow, which would be followed by a fireworks and music show in the evening. It was a beautiful sight to behold.

Being here felt like such a paradox. I loved the pageantry and the beauty and found it admirable to see people come together in celebration like this, but this very intense medieval (not the Catholic church's finest hour) vibe behind it all was just too much for me right now.

I didn't share my feelings with my daughters, but within a few hours, each of them expressed similar heavy and agitated feelings. Sonia said it first. "I can appreciate the art and the beauty and people here, but the underlying oppression is really thick in the air."

Sabrina agreed. We then speculated about what it could possibly mean. "Maybe we came here to end this heavy chapter in our own family and move on to a new, happier, lighter one. Just as this was the end of the line for the medieval knights, let this trip be the end of the line for this dark, heavy story for us as well. No more looking back. No more suffering. Let's go enjoy ourselves and just be happy to be alive."

Her words broke through the heavy veil of depression I had been fighting to get out of, like a cat struggling to get out of a bag. They struck a chord at the right moment in the right place in my heart. It *was* time now to stop fearing the future and suffering the past and all the other heavy burdens that had been suffocating me.

I realized in the most profound way that there was nothing to fear. I was not isolated. It was all in my mind. I belonged to life and was part of it. I had not been rejected and cast aside by Patrick. I had withdrawn. I was not in need of approval and acceptance by men, or by God, or by anyone anymore. No one was.

I had been dragged under by a riptide of negative self-talk: *I am not enough. I am rejected, no matter how hard I try and no matter what good I do. I am alone and not wanted.* All fears that ending my marriage had stirred up and brought to the surface.

But life was good now. I was alive and loved and free to love. And no one could stop that. I had been guided to Malta to learn this lesson. It was the end of the line for an old, old story. I needed to put it in a tomb like the ones in the cathedral. I would honor my past and let it go forever. It was heavy and sad, but now it was over. I could hardly wait to leave. I was ready to go back to Paris and create and enjoy the beautiful life *inside* that I had been watching from the outside.

Locked Out

The day after I returned from Malta, my Hay House editor from New York, Patty Gift, came to visit me. I had casually known her for years but had never spent any personal time with her until now. I had invited her to come several times since I moved here, as I knew she loved Paris as much as I did, and was delighted to have her finally accept my invitation, especially just as I commenced this new phase of my life in Paris.

The day she arrived, I had to work for a few hours in the afternoon, so she and I had lunch and afterward she set off on her own, agreeing to meet me for dinner when I finished work later that evening.

The minute I hung up the phone with clients for the day, I pulled on my boots and rushed out the door, forgetting even to put on socks, as I didn't want to keep her waiting. I took the train to the Marais, the old Jewish quarter, one of my favorite areas in Paris, which had now been taken over by chic boutiques and gay bars and was a lively mix of all that makes Paris cool and eclectic and marvelous.

We met at one of her favorite cafés, sat down to glasses of wine and delicious hors d'oeuvres, and watched the parade go by. It was marvelous fun to share Paris with someone who reminded me of all that was wonderful about being here. Being with Patty re-energized and lifted my spirit. With her enthusiastic eyes to remind me of how fortunate I was to be here, I fell in love with Paris all over again.

It was a beautiful summer night, so we decided to walk back to my apartment on the other side of Paris instead of taking the train. It was great for a few kilometers, and then a host of blisters appeared on my feet and painfully reminded me that I had no socks on under my boots.

I admitted that my wounds were overtaking me and that the walk home needed to end, and we hopped on the métro. Once out, I gingerly limped back to the apartment, barely making it as my feet were now in such agony. It was already nearing midnight and I could hardly wait to peel off my boots and give my poor feet a break. Patty was also hitting a wall. She hadn't stopped since she'd arrived that morning, and jet-lag fatigue was starting to overtake her. We were both ready to hit the sack hard.

When we arrived at my front door, I turned the key to let us in, but it didn't open. I tried several times, but the lock on the front door simply didn't release as it was supposed to. There we stood, completely bedraggled, locked out. I couldn't believe it.

I didn't know what to do. Luckily, there was still a little juice left on my phone, so I called my landlord. The phone rang and rang but no answer. Maybe she was on vacation. I didn't give up. I had no other option, as Céline, the *gardien,* was on vacation, so I couldn't reach her, and the stand-in *gardien,* a rather strange woman whom I had met only once before, didn't live here and I had no phone number by which to reach her.

To my utter relief and surprise, I eventually got through to the landlord's assistant, Benjamin, who took pity on my plight but told me there was nothing he could do tonight, as they owned the apartment I rented inside the building, but not the building itself (crazy, I know), so he could not authorize a locksmith to come and open the door without their permission. He said the only thing we could do was go to a nearby hotel for the night (which the landlord would reimburse), and he would look into it in the morning.

Barely able to walk, and feeling ridiculous to be in this predicament, I shuffled to the Radisson Hotel nearby, Patty shuffling right behind me. Unfortunately, they were sold out. We then headed over to the Intercontinental Hotel, located another block away, which was about as far as I could walk now that my blisters had become unbearable.

The entire situation was beyond absurd. I was completely embarrassed, as I hardly knew Patty and here we were in this mess. The manager of the Intercontinental, Mohammed, was a very nice gentleman to whom we explained our sorry situation. He told us he did indeed have two rooms for the night, but they were extremely expensive and he didn't want to see us spending so much money for only one short (and getting shorter) night.

I tried to explain to him that my landlord said I would be reimbursed for the room expense and that now, at one in the morning, with me in unbearable pain and Patty completely exhausted from jet lag after her jam-packed first day, we simply wanted keys to the rooms so we could call it a night.

He would not hear of it. He told us he would send his "man" over to the apartment and he would open the door for us. Expecting someone with tools and competence, after 10 long minutes of waiting, we were introduced to a young kid of only 20 or so with no idea what his manager was asking him to do. Mohammed told him to walk over with us and open the door to the building. He looked blankly at us and said, "Okay."

As we walked out the door with him and started back to my building, I turned to him and asked if he had any secret door-opening tool in his seemingly empty pockets. He said no, he had nothing. We stopped and turned back. There was no point in further insulting my feet or delaying our now serious need to lie down. We walked back to the hotel and explained to Mohammed that his guy could do nothing. We just wanted keys to our room.

Still insisting on helping us, he said there was another cheaper hotel 10 minutes away, and that we should go there. While I appreciated his chivalrous determination to help two damsels in distress, he was now annoying me beyond belief. I explained *again* that I could barely walk to the room due to my blisters, let alone another 10 minutes, then asked once more if we could please have the "friggin'" (which I didn't say but wanted to) keys to the rooms now! We were exhausted and simply wanted to go to sleep.

Finally, accepting that we were intent on staying the night, he gave us our keys and then proceeded to tell us about the amenities and Internet access our room fee entitled us to. We stopped him in his tracks. "*Mohammed,* we have no computers and our phones are nearly dead, and we will be leaving early in the morning, so there is no need for this information."

He ignored us altogether and continued to give us the full hotel amenity download as we shuffled over to the elevator, still talking as the doors to the elevator opened and we got in. His spiel continued as we pushed the button for our floor and the doors closed in his face.

Patty and I laughed out loud at this, glad to finally have keys to our rooms. I unlocked the door to my room, gingerly peeled off my now-bloody boots, and fell back on the bed, exhausted, trying to take in the absurdity of all that had just transpired.

Ten seconds later, the phone rang.

Believing it might be Patty needing something, I picked up. It was Mohammed. He wanted to finish his pitch about the Internet and amenities, which had been cut off when the elevator doors shut in his face.

"Mohammed," I said, "*listen* to me. I don't have anything to plug into the Internet. My phone is dead and I have no computer. *Now thank you and good night!*"

"Welcome back to crazy, complicated Paris," I said aloud as I started to finally relax. "I love you with all my heart and yet you frustrate and infuriate me to no end!" Then I closed my eyes and passed out. My last thought was, "I'll deal with this in the morning, hopefully."

Locked In

I slept fitfully, with dreams of being totally trapped in a corner with alligators biting at my toes, which woke me up at 7. I got dressed and placed my boots in my handbag. It was early and I was determined to get into my apartment without having to wound my severely blistered feet any more.

I left Patty sleeping and went to the lobby and checked out. Then I made my way home in my bare feet, hoping no one would see me. Fortunately, the front door to the building was now unlocked, as it always was during the day. Thank God the temporary *gardien* had arrived.

Relieved, I decided to take a shower and make myself presentable before I came down and told her about last night's nightmare situation. After I cleaned up and put on *sandals,* I went downstairs to talk with her.

When I explained the situation, to my surprise her reaction was an intense, *"Ce n'est pas ma faute!"* meaning, "It's not my fault!"

I explained that of course I understood it was not her *fault*, I just couldn't open the door with my key when I came home last night. Apparently the electronic release for the lock was broken and the key didn't work. Someone needed to come immediately to repair it before the day was over. I simply couldn't be locked out again, as I had been last night.

She became completely flummoxed and said she had no way to call someone as she was only the *temporary gardien* and did not have the authority to get it fixed. Not believing what I was hearing, I calmly insisted, once again, that there was no way she could leave me in this situation and that she absolutely *had* to find someone to come and repair the lock today. As acting *gardien* she was indeed the *only* one who had the authority to fix it and must.

She got more and more hysterical by the minute and insisted that she was not able to address the problem, again reminding me that she was only the *temporary gardien*. Meanwhile, I became more and more insistent that she not only could, but also absolutely *would* address the problem today *because* she was the acting *gardien*.

Then I called my landlord's assistant, Benjamin, again, while standing in her presence and left an urgent message on his voice mail that he must call her and persuade her to get someone over to repair the lock and end this stupid situation.

The acting *gardien* now screamed and called me a fascist American brat, which totally took me by surprise and almost made me laugh, as it was so out of left field. I chose to ignore her. I simply stated *again* (while at the same time restraining my overwhelming impulse to lunge at her and shake her silly) that she had to call a repairman immediately and get the door fixed today, before she left for the weekend. Being the only tenant in the building who came and went at night, I needed to be able to do just that without question.

She said Céline was in Spain, and she couldn't call her. I insisted that Céline could be called and that she *must* call her now. She screamed again, and boy did I want to as well! But I knew it would do me no good whatsoever.

Finally she angrily agreed to *try* to call someone to come look at the lock, but she made no promise that it would be repaired today.

Exasperated, I mustered every shred of self-control in me and said, "*Merci,*" then calmly walked back to my apartment, shut the door, and screamed. This was so stupid! I called Benjamin again and insisted that he follow up with her so I could be assured the lock would be fixed today, before he, too, took off for the weekend.

Shortly after, Patty arrived and I gave her the update. A few minutes later, I received a phone call from the temporary *gardien* that someone would be coming today after all, hopefully before she left at 5, but there were no promises. Then she informed me that Monday was a holiday and that she would not be here then.

Patty took a shower and then we sat down to discuss the situation. As we spoke, it suddenly occurred to me that if the door was not fixed, not only could we again get locked out, but we could also potentially get *locked in* for the entire long weekend. This was just too much—I couldn't believe it!

Both of us being take-charge American women, we decided this was not going to happen. We hatched a plan right then and there to go to BHV and buy some heavy tape and putty and jimmy the lock to keep it from closing in case the crazy temporary *gardien* had any notion of leaving before the lock got fixed. Since I worked again in a few hours, we dashed out the door and headed to the métro straight away. We were on a mission.

An hour later we had secured heavy-duty tape and putty and were back in the apartment, prepared to stealthily do our dirty work. In another 30 minutes I had to begin work. Patty said, "I'm going to go down and see what the situation is." I warned her that the *gardien* was crazy and to be prepared, but she said, "I'm a New Yorker, Sonia. I can handle her."

Five minutes later Patty texted me. "Oh my God! This woman is crazy! I'm not leaving here until she gets the door fixed."

Apparently Patty, not realizing the *gardien*'s door led to her apartment and not an office, simply opened it and walked in. This sent the temporary *gardien* into an apoplectic fit.

"How dare you just walk in?" she screamed, and demanded that Patty leave immediately. Patty said, "No. I'm not leaving until the door is fixed and that is that."

Suddenly it was a showdown at the OK Corral. Patty stood her ground, as did the *gardien*. All of this was being relayed to me in real time via text while I was on the phone with clients.

Patty didn't budge. Soon a repairman showed up. This made no difference, Patty said. Until the door was fixed, she wasn't moving.

The electrician started checking out the problem, while the temporary *gardien* raged at Patty. Patty ignored her. The workman raised an eyebrow to all of this, as he was only three feet away, then started to look into the box that controlled the electronic lock mechanism. After he poked around in there a bit, he said the wiring was very old and had simply given out, and set about doing what he could to repair it.

In the meantime the *gardien* went from crazy anger to crying, and suddenly started downloading on Patty about what a disaster her life was. She said she had cancer and had lost her job as a designer because she was too old now. She complained about how everyone was against her and how Americans were spoiled brats and on and on and on.

Surprised by all of this, Patty began in her sketchy French to now comfort and reassure the *gardien,* texting me along the way that the saga downstairs had just gotten more complicated, *but* the door was on its way to being fixed, finally. Hurray!

All the while, I was on the phone with clients, only grasping bits and pieces of this absurd scenario. Hearing that the lock was in the process of being fixed, however, I texted, "Way to go, Patty! Hang in there until we know we are free and clear to enter and leave without a problem."

An hour later, just as I finished work, Patty returned, triumphant. The door lock was fixed, she reported, and the temporary *gardien* was now Patty's friend. This called for a celebration! I grabbed my purse and keys and we headed out the door.

"Welcome to the *real* Paris," I said to Patty. "It is so absurd living here that you either laugh or go crazy." We decided to laugh. And laugh and laugh. And yet, after all of this, we also felt compassion for the temporary *gardien,* whom we now called Madame Crazy. Daily doses of this kind of frustration would make anyone lose it over time. We stopped and bought her a present of espresso coffee, which she had told Patty she loved with her cigarettes. Since I lived here and would no doubt encounter her again, it was important to make a peace offering to show her my appreciation for getting the door fixed, even if it did take a lot of drama and heavy persuasion to do so. It was Paris, after all, and this was the correct thing to do.

Going to sleep that night, I reflected on how this experience mirrored the fear I had been carrying about being trapped here, simultaneously locked into my lease and emotionally locked out by Parisians. But then I realized that now, thanks to my own determination (and Patty's fabulous help), the door to Paris was freely opened to me. I could come and go as I pleased and no one, and not one thing, could stop me now, both where I lived and in life in general. Hallelujah!

Dancing with Mr. Bean

After Malta and Patty's visit, I resolved to make meeting people and making friends my top priority. I decided that it was time to start going out, even dating, although my heart was only halfway into this. I wasn't really interested in having a boyfriend, but I did want to have some playmates to do things with in Paris, so I opened myself up to all possibilities.

This led me to meeting Victor, an acquaintance of a friend who lived in New York. He was French, worked in television here in Paris, was near my age, and loved to dance, she said, and he would be interested in meeting me. That was all I needed to make a date with him. He reached out by text and we agreed to meet at a nearby French nightclub, the Matignon, just off the Champs-Elysées, and go dancing. Having not been to a nightclub in years, I was looking forward to this new adventure.

Since the French go out very late, our date began at midnight. By that hour all I really wanted to do was put on my pj's and go to sleep, but I had to push past my resistance and show up. *This is all part of letting go of the old me and letting a new me step in,* I told myself. Besides, tomorrow morning I could sleep in. With this thought, I rallied and set off.

We met at the lounge above the disco. At first glance, Victor looked like Rowan Atkinson, the British actor and comedian who plays Mr. Bean in the most hilarious British comedies. Only I soon found out, unlike Mr. Bean, he wasn't very funny.

We decided to have a glass of champagne and get to know each other a bit before going down to the disco. I tried to make light conversation, but he was way too intense for that. No matter what silly, light-hearted comment I made, he took it as an invitation to display his intellectual prowess, going off on a tangent for many minutes, rife with historical facts, political facts, and just plain boring opinions, most of which were difficult to follow as it was so loud in there. Oh well, I didn't necessarily come to make a philosophical friend, I told myself. I just came to dance, and apparently this was something he loved to do, so I hung in there.

After an hour of soliloquies, he finally suggested we go to the disco, which I was grateful to do, as it was now nearly 1:30 in the morning and I was fading fast.

To my surprise, the dance floor was nearly empty. Victor, noticing my reaction, leaned in and said it was because it was still a bit early for dancing. Discos normally don't get going until well after 2 A.M. in Paris, he said. That didn't deter him, however. He shuffled right onto the dance floor and began to let loose.

To my delight he was a great dancer and *really* strutted his stuff. I joined right in, as I *love* to dance. Within 60 seconds I was totally re-energized. This promised to be fun! And it was, for about five minutes. Then I realized that Victor was actually *not* dancing *with* me, or even dancing in his own flow, but was performing *for* me and was annoyed that I wasn't watching his show.

He danced right up to me again and again, trying to get my attention, and then rip-roared into an outrageous routine for me to applaud and appreciate. The first few times he did this, I laughed and applauded. But soon it got really annoying. I wanted to let loose and dance, not act as his personal audience.

I decided to ignore him and just have fun dancing on my own, but he would have none of it. He kept upping the ante with his dance moves to get my attention, and soon he was nearly doing splits to hold my gaze exclusively on him.

What the hell is he doing? I wondered, as I tried to keep dancing and enjoying myself. *Is he for real or is this just a French thing?*

I danced away as the floor began to get more and more crowded, but he danced right after me, strolling across the floor like John Travolta in *Saturday Night Fever*. It was surreal. Soon I found myself danced into a corner, in front of a back service bar. Sure enough, he came watusi-ing up to me, his necktie now off and swinging in the air as if to scream, "Pay attention to ME!" which I now decided I would *not* do, no matter what.

As I defiantly danced to the beat of my own drummer, he fought for my attention ever more furiously with even wilder antics. There was a curtain strung across the service bar, which he proceeded to dance himself into, rolling up in the curtain, then rolling back, and then up again. I laughed at this new level of desperation, but he mistakenly took my reaction as one of encouragement. He then began to dance down one side of the service bar and then disappear behind it, only to pop out on the other side and roll up into the curtain again. It was then I realized I really *was* dancing with Mr. Bean!

Finally, I gave up trying to get the message across to him that I just wanted to dance and not be held hostage to paying exclusive attention to him, and I strolled off the dance floor altogether. I went over to the bar and ordered a Perrier. I was hot, exhausted, and completely over this entire ridiculous experience. Missing the cue entirely, Mr. Bean danced over to the bar and *kept dancing* in my face while I stared at him and drank my water. Then I put my glass down and said, "Good night, Victor. I'm ready to go home now," and headed for the exit.

He danced me to the exit, danced me upstairs, and danced me all the way outside. I couldn't believe this guy. He then said he would walk me home, but I was sure that he meant he would *dance* me home. I panicked. I lived only a 15-minute walk away but couldn't bear this for one more second. I begged off, saying I was too tired to walk and would prefer to jump into a taxi, of which thankfully there were many right there. Then, before he could object, I kissed him quickly on both cheeks *à la française,* said a speedy "thank you" and "good night," and escaped into the cab, slamming the door behind me. I then avoided looking out the window, as I'm sure I would have seen him dancing after the cab if he so much as caught a sliver of eye contact from me.

I laughed all the way home. "Good night, Mr. Bean," I said aloud as I jumped into bed. "Nice dancing with you."

Ballet in Tuscany

Shortly after Mr. Bean and I parted ways, another friend (or rather, an acquaintance from the U.K.) insisted I meet a man, William, who, according to her, was the perfect companion for me. He was French, single, a total gentleman, very successful, well-traveled, and very eager to meet me. "A total catch, Sonia. You are in for a treat."

Suspicious but willing, I agreed to meet as long as he didn't consider it a "romantic" date, but rather just a chance to make a friend. He called me the next day, and we had a lively conversation on the phone, partially thanks to his ability to speak perfect and elegant English. I liked him a lot.

He told me he worked in the energy field, but his first and true wish was to be a ballet dancer. *Oh wow,* I thought. *Another dancer!* But soon after, our conversation moved on to creativity and writing and travel and love of life. He was easy to talk to, so when he invited me to dinner the following Saturday, I gladly accepted. We agreed to meet at 8 P.M. in the Marais.

The weather was gorgeous, so I decided to walk to the restaurant to take advantage of the beautiful night. When I arrived he was sitting alone at an outside table, wearing a rose-colored sweater casually draped over his shoulders the way only an older, conservative French man can do and not look completely effeminate.

He wasn't very tall and I fairly towered over him when we first greeted one another, but that was okay. When I sat down, he immediately ordered two glasses of champagne, which I found to be very classy and "French" of him. We toasted to new friendship and proceeded to begin to learn a little more about each other.

After we ordered (he insisted on ordering for both of us) and were served our salads, he told me he had a "big surprise" for me. Hearing this was a surprise in itself as I had only just met him—so what on earth could be the surprise?

He told me that he had heard I was intuitive and, well, in fact, so was he. So following our initial conversation, after learning how we were both dancers and writers (albeit he only in the beginning stages), he followed his intuition and rented a villa in Tuscany for the entire month of October, feeling it would be a wonderful experience for both of us to share.

I almost choked on my lettuce. Not sure I had heard him correctly, I regained my composure and asked him to please repeat what he had just said. He laughed and said he thought I would be not only surprised, but also thrilled. Then once again, this time taking my hand in his, which was very uncomfortable, he said he had arranged to rent a villa in Tuscany for the entire month of October, feeling it would be the perfect thing for both of us to share.

I looked at him incredulously. "William," I said, laughing, "I don't even know you. I can't go to Tuscany with you for a month in October."

"Why not?" he answered, brushing off my objection. "We are not young. We must trust our intuition, as you suggest, and take the chance for love."

I had to appreciate William's wildly romantic, optimistic, but completely delusional whim. "I'm really sorry, William," I answered. "I simply won't be able to do that. Not only do I not know you, I have to lead workshops in the States in October. I can't get away for a month, even if I were taken by the idea."

"Another time is better?" he persisted.

"No, William. It's not. You and I are strangers."

"Only for now." He smiled and reached for my hand again.

I smiled back, pulling my hand free, and again said, "I'm sorry, William. It's such a beautiful offer, but I have to turn it down."

He looked quite surprised that I had declined. "Are you *certain* that you do not want to accept my invitation?" he pushed further.

"Yes, William, I am."

Things had suddenly turned very awkward, as we hadn't even had our main course yet, and I now had to endure his disappointment for the rest of the evening. I gulped down the rest of my champagne.

All during dinner, I marveled at his audacity and secretly wondered if, had he been more attractive to me, I might have given him a different answer. I immediately chastised myself for being so superficial and tried my best to make casual conversation. My rejection seemed to take the wind out of his conversational sails for the rest of the meal, as his offer did mine, and our efforts to keep the mood light were not very successful.

After dinner William offered to take me home in his car, but I insisted on walking home instead, as it was a beautiful night. Truthfully, I did not want to get into a car with him as I feared I would feel trapped. Maybe that was an overreaction on my part, but given his complete lack of appropriate boundaries, I was not going to question my instinct. He moved much too fast, and I just wanted to get out of there.

But he had other ideas. He absolutely *insisted* on walking over to the Île Saint-Louis to get some ice cream at his favorite place, Amorino, before we said good night.

Feeling badly for rejecting his Tuscany offer, I relented and agreed. I didn't want to be unkind, and he was a nice guy, if more than a bit presumptuous. The night was still young and a walk was harmless enough, I told myself, but underneath it all, I felt pressured by what he wanted.

We continued on to Amorino, only to find it had just closed 10 minutes earlier. "I guess it's not our night for ice cream," I said, trying to be cheerful, taking my hand back firmly and placing it in my pocket. He seemed really upset that Amorino was not to be had, but I sensed it was more than that. His entire fantasy was coming to a disappointing end.

The entire evening had been so over-the-top that I just wanted it to end. He once again offered to take me home, but just then we were standing right in front of a métro stop, so I declined. I think this time he was relieved that I did.

I kissed both of his cheeks and said, "Thank you so much for the lovely evening, William. Enjoy writing in Tuscany. Good night." Then I ran down the stairs and caught the next train.

Riding home, I tried to absorb what had just transpired. I couldn't fault William for his optimism or his romantic generous notions. He was lonely and understandably wanted companionship. Who among us doesn't want that at some point? It just wasn't meant to be for us.

"Too bad," I said to myself as I left the métro. "A month in a Tuscan villa does sound romantic."

Off the Beaten Track

In the interest of furthering my new intention to establish friendships in Paris, one day I spontaneously decided to join a Meetup group offering a tour of street art on a Sunday afternoon in a neighborhood I had not yet explored, the 13th *quartier* near the Buttes-Chaumont.

The group arranged to meet at a quintessential old-school Parisian café, which I loved the minute I walked in the door. It had beautiful Belle Époque etched glass and painted walls lined with red banquettes, with small café tables scattered throughout the room. An Edith Piaf recording was playing in the background. Along the entire length of one wall was a classic zinc bar with a few stools in front of it and an unusually cheerful guy working behind it. He smiled when I entered and pointed to the right. There I saw what had to be our Meetup group sitting in the middle of the café around several tables that had been pushed together, allowing people to chat with one another while waiting for everyone to arrive. I was happy to see people of all ages gathered around and engaged in lively conversation.

I sat next to a young Chinese-American woman from New York named Louise, who was very eager to chat. Twentysomething and newly arrived in Paris, she immediately told me she had long dreamed of moving to Paris and had finally made it happen. She was on a mission to find and live with a Parisian boyfriend, so had been to at least two to three Meetup groups a day since she arrived. After only two weeks in town, she had already received *two* offers from young French men to move in with them and was debating which one would be the better option. We talked for a while as she mentally tried to sort out her dilemma, and finally, just before we were about to begin the tour, she announced she would go with the guy who had the more comfortable place to live, which she hadn't yet had the chance to see as she was so busy with all her Meetup groups. She didn't want to rush her decision though, she said. While the two guys she met seemed okay, she was going to attend at least 10 more Meetup groups in case she met any other male candidates for the boyfriend-and-free-apartment position before she made her choice. "You never know who I'll meet," she said, not the least bit worried about establishing any kind of real connection before moving in. "I know what men like: sex and flattery, and I'm super good at both. I like fun and comfort, so I'll just need to see which guy has the most to offer me."

I respected her direct, if totally superficial and somewhat dangerous approach to living in Paris. It seemed so much easier than my complicated thoroughly-heal-the-deepest-wounds-in-my-soul-before-I-start-even-making-friends-and-begin-again approach to being here. I just shook my head when listening to her, wondering if life really *could* be that simple. She seemed pretty happy, if a little manic. She then offered to send me a list of Meetup groups for "older" people in case I wanted to try her approach to getting a new boyfriend, assuming that was what I was looking for. She had attended several Meetups thinking they were for her but found out she was with the wrong age group.

"There were a lot of nice men there, Sonia. Some were weird and most were short, bald, and fat but still . . . I'm happy to pass this information along."

I thanked her for her generosity. "Sure, why not?" I said, and gave her my e-mail. By then it was time to go.

I found myself walking alongside a man named Luigi, a fifty-something street artist from Florence who specialized in what he called "Trash Art." Trash Art, he explained, was a form of street art he created that involved drawing on discarded items left on the street that were waiting to be picked up by the garbagemen.

"That way I'll never get arrested," he chuckled, happy that he figured out how to beat the system. He had come prepared to make his mark in Paris with 10 colored permanent markers sticking out of his front jacket pocket.

He was in luck the day we set off on our tour, as we happened upon a lot of trash. There was an old mattress on one street we walked down, a stack of wooden boxes piled high on another, and a huge broken-down dresser with drawers on the ground on another street we walked along. Each of these discoveries made him squeal with delight and then frantically get to work with his markers.

Amazingly, he was able to whip out his markers and work his razzmatazz on all of these items in a matter of seconds and still keep up with the group, even hearing a thing or two the guide was saying. Offering a secondary tour of his own alongside ours, he explained to whoever would listen (mostly just me) that being a "true" street artist required that you work as fast as lightning so you don't get caught. His drawing seemed pretty amateurish, but I loved his commitment to it and fully encouraged him to carry on with his dream.

The tour officially started about 15 feet from the café, where on a single corner our guide pointed out tiled art, spray-painted art, stenciled art, art on paper that had been slapped on the sides of buildings, art on light posts and trash cans and even the sidewalk itself. I was a bit startled to realize that I might never have noticed most of it had she not pointed it out. To see it you had to look up, look sideways, and look in places your eye generally doesn't travel to when walking down the street. It expanded my perception in every direction. We continued our tour for another two or three kilometers around the area. Most of the art we saw was really fantastic and a lot of it was silly and amusing as well. I was really impressed with it all.

Our guide, Aurélie, a 35-year-old street artist herself who had been at it for over 20 years, was terrific and funny and very informative as she introduced us to some of the more famous street artists' work in the area.

"They all work undercover, by night," she said. "It is against the law to deface buildings here in Paris, as it is in most places, so the game of cat and mouse between the police and the street artists is of course part of the romance of it all."

She also told us that the police keep entire dossiers filled with photos of the work of various street artists around Paris, which they often keep for years, so if an artist is ever caught, he or she is fined for all of his or her work and not just what he or she is caught doing in the moment. The total could amount to hundreds of thousands of euros, so it was a very dangerous craft. Once I learned about street art on that tour and whose work was whose, I began to notice more and more of it all over Paris. After the tour I felt very "in the Parisian know" and much more connected to the many layers of reality going on here at once. I just had to look up and in a new direction and a whole new world opened up before my eyes. It was a lesson that applied not just to enjoying street art, but to noticing and enjoying more of everything in Paris now. Especially the people.

Walking home I was overwhelmed with just how blessed I felt to be here. The city was beautiful and fascinating, and these nuances made it all the more exciting and mysterious. More importantly, my days were now spent in living color. I wasn't unconscious. I wasn't on autopilot. I wasn't lost in my head. I was wide awake, fully present, and loving my life, and that was the greatest gift of all.

Opening My Heart

Once I decided that Paris *was* truly my new home and allowed myself to feel that I *did* belong—despite being an American who liked to hug instead of make air kisses, to laugh out loud and be transparent, to listen to my intuition and believe in miracles and regularly talk to God, to not wear white button-down shirts and black blazers and only occasionally remember to put on red lipstick, to walk around town in my Adidas sneakers instead of feet-destroying high heels, to smile at people from ear to ear instead of appearing aloof and disinterested, and to drink champagne *without* ice cubes and simply be myself in this marvelous, magical city—the door to making *real* friends *finally* began to crack open.

The first real friend I made was a woman named Lilou Mace, whom I already actually knew, as she was a video journalist who blogged about all things spiritual and had interviewed me several times over the past eight years.

Lilou used to live in America, but, like me, had recently moved to Paris. She reached out shortly after she arrived and we instantly became friends. Lilou was the perfect friend to have as she was French-born but raised in the U.S., so she embodied the best of both cultures. Lilou was as deeply committed to conscious spiritual living as I was, as well, so our time spent together was filled with deep conversation and soul exploration, as well as delicious French food, champagne, and lots of loud American-style laughter.

In between slurping down oysters and drinking white wine, we began to plot how best to awaken intuition in French people. Lilou proposed we write a workbook and create an online course together, and I agreed, as it sounded like great fun. Our co-creation was called *The 100-Day Challenge for Developing Your Intuition,* a workbook introducing one intuitive tool a day for 100 days. Lilou got a French publisher to take it on, and in a few short months, it became a reality. Soon after it was published, Lilou set up a tour of several cities in France where we both promoted it and taught workshops together.

As we encouraged French people to relax more and trust their vibes, a theme spontaneously presented itself to us. Soon our mantra in these workshops became *"Liberez les fesses,"* literally meaning, "Free your tight-butts."

Lilou and I marched around the stage like people on strike, chanting "Liberez les fesses." Loving it, our audiences spontaneously joined in the chant, and our workshops burst into fun and laughter everywhere we went.

In addition to becoming a great friend and creative collaborator, Lilou was also a social butterfly who made friends everywhere she went. Tagging along with her, I met many other wonderful people, one of whom was Marion Ross. Marion was another American spiritual teacher and writer who lived part-time in Paris, part-time in Grasse in the south of France, and part-time in the U.S. Standing all of five-foot-two and originally from Rogers Park in Chicago, not far from where I used to live, Marion was a positive and powerful force to be reckoned with, a conscious, direct, loving, generous, spiritual *compadre* with whom I instantly bonded. She quickly befriended me, inviting me often to join her for long walks and great dinners filled with heartfelt conversation, for which I was very grateful.

Like an angel dropping directly out of the sky, Marion quickly became my champion, my cheerleader, my sounding board, my witness, my coach, and my personal healer. Having had an apartment very near mine for more than 20 years, Marion understood full well the particular, and often ridiculous, challenges that came with living in Paris as an outsider and making it feel like home. She knew how difficult and lonely Paris can be at first, yet understood how worth the effort it was to stay. She, like me, loved the beauty; the food; the slower, more graceful, gracious, and sensitive way of living that this glorious and complicated city insisted upon. She understood the culture shock and how easy it was to become discouraged when trying to find friends and build a life and meaningful community here, especially when Parisians tended to be aloof and insulated.

Marion especially helped me to stop judging myself for having fallen into such a state of despair over the summer.

"It happens, Sonia," she said. "Paris is so alluring, but it is not easy to find and establish deeper connections with spiritually minded people here. That takes time, patience, prayer, and persistence, all of which you have, so be nice to yourself," she insisted. "It will get easier."

"Thank you for the reassurance and comforting words," I answered.

"Others will show up," she said. "Trust me. You are changing so much now, and new people will step in who match your new energy. It is the way things work."

Marion was right. I had just totally deconstructed not only my old life, but also the old me, and like a caterpillar slowly turning into a butterfly, I was just barely emerging from the "mush" state of my own metamorphosis. I was deeply grateful to be reassured and reminded by Marion that I wasn't crazy, I wasn't stuck, I wasn't an outsider, I wasn't a spiritual failure, and that, above all, transformation is *always* a messy affair and can be slow, so I should not judge myself harshly.

Marion reminded me that underneath the beautiful *"vie en rose"* we both enjoyed, Paris is a tough place in which to undergo inner transformation. The soul of Paris is not at all sentimental. It's blunt, direct, and can even be quite harsh, not in a mean way, just brutally honest.

We discussed how intense it is to live here, but how it is worth it because you become more authentic the longer you stay. Paris has no tolerance for or patience with anything fake or cheap or ugly, and that includes what is inside of you, as well. I believe that is the secret gift of Paris and the real reason it casts such a spell on people all over the world. It *demands* that you recognize and insist on the most beautiful version of life, inside and out. Like polishing a diamond, living in Paris casts off the shadow and forces your true light to shine. And the process hurts.

Marion became a steady companion and grounding force as I settled ever more fully into my life here. She also jump-started me into consciously calling in the kinds of people I really wanted to meet. I began to pray for new and uplifting people to show up, and my prayers started being answered.

Soon after Lilou introduced me to Marion, I met a great guy named David Brower. A fellow American who had moved to Paris in his early 20s and had stayed ever since, making it his home with his French wife, Agnès, David was a master at celebrating all that was beautiful and sensuous and delicious and creative. He was a talented chef, a conscious connector, and a purveyor of authentic human experiences. David offered a sort of Cirque du Soleil for the senses by way of exquisite, intimate events he called the "Sensorial Experience," which he and his wife held not only in Paris but around the world. They were full-day affairs designed to feed the body, mind, heart, and soul. A true master of ceremonies, during these events David invited people to savor delicious food and wine while discovering their voice in song, their rhythm in dance, their expression in making art, and their joy in sharing authentic communication with creative and mindful others.

David and I instantly bonded over tea on the back *terrasse* of his wonderful apartment in the 15th *quartier,* which had come about by way of an out-of-the-blue e-mail invitation he had sent me after a mutual friend in the U.K. suggested we meet. I felt he was another angel sent by God to brighten up my life and help make me feel at home.

While attending a wonderful dinner party at David's the following month, I met his close friend Butzi, a wildly creative professional magician, writer, filmmaker, and creativity igniter, and his gorgeous girlfriend, Diana, an accomplished chef specializing in her native Cambodian food. Butzi was hilarious and made me laugh really hard, he and I sharing the same style of super-silly humor.

Next Dominic showed up, an unusually open man. He worked for a big European tech company and had a very demanding job, yet had raised his three young children by himself when his wife suddenly divorced him and left them all. He also helped raise his sister's three sons after she, too, experienced a difficult and painful divorce of her own. Dominic was one of five brothers and one sister raised in a big Catholic family similar to mine. We talked a lot about the trials and tribulations of that and shared a deep love of prayer and God and angels and Mother Mary. Dominic had a wilder side, as well, which found its expression through his love of motorcycles. One night while we were out to dinner together, he pulled out his phone and showed me photos of two bikes and told me he had been debating which one to buy next. I told him that the next time I saw him, it had to be on one of the two bikes, with an extra helmet in hand so he could take me for a ride. We had a deal.

Dominic understood me. He understood my spirituality, my humor, and my transparency. He also understood my pain, as he too had had to rebuild his life after a sudden divorce. I learned from him just by listening to the stories of all that he went through and how he found his new normal after his life fell apart. As he drove me home one evening after sharing a wonderful dinner and walk along the Seine, he spontaneously said, "Sonia, there just comes a moment when you decide it's time to be happy and that is all." I had that moment in Malta, but it was good to hear it again.

My next new friend was another hugely creative woman living in Paris, but originally from Australia, named Carla. I met her through Sabrina, who was looking online for gluten-free recipes one day and happened upon Carla's blog on gluten-free living in

Paris. After reading her blog, Sabrina saw that Carla was also a photographer and looked at her website, which was filled with absolutely gorgeous photos. Since I needed new photos for my website, Sabrina forwarded her information on to me and I gave her call.

Not only was Carla an incredibly talented photographer, she was also an intuitive, warm, genuine person whom I became friends with after our super-fun photo shoot. She, too, knew the challenges of moving to Paris as a foreigner, and we laughed till we cried, sharing the trials and tribulations of adjusting to this wonderful, yet crazily complicated city. We especially bonded over the stress we had both faced when securing our official *cartes de sejour* at the Préfecture de Police, which we needed in order to stay in France after our visas expired. The paperwork alone was monumental, and it seemed the people who worked at the Préfecture hated most of the human race. I told her how a woman who worked there had yelled at me to stop looking at her while I was waiting my turn, even though I had only casually glanced her way. Carla was sure she'd had the pleasure of being yelled at by the same woman for the same reason. I said the next time I needed to renew my *carte de sejour*, I would wear sunglasses so no one could see my eyes until my turn was called.

Before I knew it, fall was well under way and my cup was starting to "runneth over" with all these new and marvelously creative, warm, openhearted people from all over the world. True friendships started blossoming from all these introductions, and I began to sense that my life in Paris was *finally* beginning to become the beautiful experience I had so desperately yearned for when I first came here almost two years earlier.

The more I slowed down, the more grounded and committed I became in my decision to bury the past and truly *be* here, the more I opened my heart fully once again and started inviting and allowing people in, the more great people showed up. I had turned a corner and was now on my way to belonging to Paris, and it to me, at last.

The Christmas Party

Before I knew it, it was Christmastime. From the gorgeous decorations lighting up the streets and boulevards to the Christmas markets popping up along the far end of the Champs-Elysées and in the various neighborhoods to the Christmas music pouring through the loudspeakers of every single store in town to the mobs of tourists trudging up and down the streets with cameras and shopping bags, craning their necks in all directions to take in the countless beautiful sights, holiday fever was everywhere.

Paris never looked more gorgeous. In the middle of every plaza was a decorated Christmas tree, and every florist had trees, wreaths, and holiday bouquets displayed on the sidewalk. Unlike a year ago, when Paris and I were still so wounded, this year we were both feeling happier.

I bundled up and enjoyed long walks throughout the city every free moment I had and started to fall in love with Paris all over again. I decided to explore new neighborhoods, as I had become a bit complacent and had not ventured much beyond my own *quartier* in recent weeks and felt my world constricting. I was ready to expand once again.

One day, while wandering home through the festively decorated market street, rue Montorgueil, in the 2nd *quartier,* which I rarely visited, looking at all the delicious Christmas foods displayed in the shops and open market stalls, I suddenly had the urge to throw a Christmas party for all of my new friends.

At first the idea scared me a little, as I knew there were unspoken but somewhat strict rules for properly entertaining in Paris, about which I knew nothing. I wanted to celebrate, but I didn't want to embarrass myself by not doing it right.

I then thought of another problem. I didn't cook at all, so didn't have anything I could serve my guests. Because of that liability (which I had already resolved I *would* correct with cooking classes in the new year), I immediately (and wisely) ruled out the possibility of having a *dinner* party. The more I thought about it as I walked along, feeling the holiday mood in the air and realizing that none of my new friends were judgmental in the least, the more I thought that perhaps it would be possible to have a cocktail, champagne, and hors d'oeuvres party. I could manage this because I could have it *catered*.

I wouldn't even be embarrassed about that because I knew Parisians got frozen hors d'oeuvres from a company called Picard all the time and served them at cocktail parties without apology. Real hors d'oeuvres that didn't come from Picard would be downright classy.

Besides, the idea of throwing a party felt really fun. I loved Christmas and wanted to celebrate. After thinking it over as I walked for a few more blocks, I decided to go for it.

Once I made the decision to have a catered party, I realized that it could still be difficult to find the right catering company and order the right hors d'oeuvres. But since I had already made up my mind to have the party, I didn't let that stop me. I simply e-mailed David, the master party thrower, and elicited his help in finding a caterer and choosing a proper menu.

David was immediately on board and got to it right away. While he was organizing the food, I began to make up the guest list. I invited all my new friends—David and Agnès; Butzi and Diana; Marion; Dominic; Carla and her Italian husband, Francesco; and Lilou and her fiancé, Mikael—and hoped they could all attend. As I made up my list, I was amazed at how quickly my life had changed

I decided to have my Christmas cocktail party on a Thursday evening from 8 to 10 P.M. That way people could come after work and it wouldn't conflict with any potential weekend holiday plans they might already have, as it was getting late in the season. David thought that was a great idea, especially since all of *his* holiday weekends were already committed.

I also got the urge to ask David to invite some more of his friends to my "cocktail," as it was simply called here. Why not? I wanted to open my heart and home as wide as I could and welcome even more people in to celebrate together and enjoy this marvelous time of year.

With David as my helper, the date was set, the invitations were sent, and the plans got under way. Upon hearing about the party, Sabrina surprised me and said she would come from London to help, which only made it more festive.

She showed up the day before the party and together we set about decorating my Zen-looking apartment with colorful pillows, bright plants, Christmas lights, and scented candles. We played Christmas music while we strung lights and sang Christmas songs as we ran around Paris getting last-minute sweets and cheeses, more champagne, and chocolates.

It was hard to believe what a long way I'd come from where I was only four months earlier in August, when I cried day after day, wondering if it had been a terrible mistake to move here after all. Now I was getting ready to celebrate at my own party. It actually felt like a miracle.

At 6 P.M. on the night of the event, the catered food arrived. I didn't even know what we were serving, as David had picked it all out. We soon learned I had ordered seven small courses, including tiny salmon sandwiches, pots of fresh vegetables in sour cream, shrimp on a stick, miniature puff pastries stuffed with eggplant and tomato, tiny little soups, vegetable burgers, and raspberry *tartes* for dessert. The hors d'oeuvres came with their own tiny little serving forks, spoons, napkins, and trays, all ready to go. The caterer said all I had to do was bring them out, one course at a time, and smile. That I could easily do.

Expecting everyone at 8 P.M., Sabrina and I nervously put the last touches on the apartment, then slipped into our best party dresses and high-fived each other, saying, "Let's do this thing!"

At 7:45 David arrived with Agnès and a friend of his named Marc, from Marseille. Marc was a great guy and immediately set up a bar for our guests on the dining-room table and opened up some champagne and put it in an ice bucket. All the while he chatted merrily about his life, his family, living in Marseille, and meeting me. In only minutes he felt like a longtime friend.

Shortly after 8, the other guests started arriving, both my own as well as David's friends. At first I was nervous, as most people didn't know one another, but those fears flew out the door in no time. With a little music and champagne, and those great hors d'oeuvres, everyone relaxed soon enough and the evening got livelier and livelier by the minute.

At midnight the party was still going strong, although it was only meant to be a two-hour cocktail event. It was a great success—no one wanted to go home—and I loved every minute of it.

We air-kissed and American-hugged the last of our guests good night at 1 in the morning. Sabrina and I wandered back into the living room, plopped down next to each other on the sofa, and stared out the huge windows in front of us, full of satisfaction. Feeling happy and pleased that everyone had enjoyed themselves, and delighted to have met so many new people—not to mention hugely proud that I had *actually* thrown my first Parisian party—I breathed a sigh of relief and contentment. Butzi even said, on the way out the door, that the evening was *"Pas mal,"* meaning "Not bad." According to him, this was a high compliment in France.

From arriving in a completely frantic state at the Old Lady in shell-shocked Paris less than two years ago, huddled with Sabrina for both warmth and emotional comfort in a freezing cold room, to now having a beautiful home and celebrating with gorgeous friends from around the world, all I could do was shout out loud, "Thank you, Jesus!"

My old life and old self were dead, their ashes still scattering in my memory and settling into my soul. The darkest nights were now behind me. I was finally resurrecting into a brand-new life as a brand-new me, and it felt wonderful. It was as though I was just waking up from a long, dark night of the soul and stepping fully into the light once again.

Sitting there with Sabrina, thinking about the changes that the past two years had brought for both of us, I realized that transformation does not happen all at once. Even if it begins with a huge shift, as it did for me, it unfolds thereafter one small moment, one small experience, one small "aha," one small honest reflection, one small act of forgiveness at a time—mixed in with lots and lots of tears and laughter. My transformation was far from over. My future was a complete blur. But at this moment, life was wonderful, and if I stayed in the moment, I knew intuitively all would continue to be well.

I also deeply appreciated just how Paris had been the perfect landing on my soul's journey over the past few difficult years and felt in my soul that we shared lifetimes and lifetimes and lifetimes of healing together. For all of her quirks, arrogance, and demands, she was my safe place, my truth serum, and my solid ground. This city's beauty and regal, unapologetic sense and love of who she was allowed me to embody and embrace even more of that in myself.

There was a little champagne in the last bottle left over from the party. I got out two glasses and filled them, then toasted with Sabrina. "To our bright futures, Sabrina. May all our dreams keep coming true."

"Amen, Mom," she said. "I'll toast to that."

And then, just before going to bed, I shared one more thing.

"By the way, Sabrina," I said, smiling from ear to ear before heading to bed, "do you want to see my new white shirt? This time I think I *finally* found one I like."

She laughed and said, "Give it up, Mom. You are *never* going to be a white-button-down-shirt-wearing Frenchwoman."

"That is so true, Sabrina," I said, laughing. "I finally got that. I don't even want a button-down make-me-look-*French* white shirt anymore. Now close your eyes."

"*Tah-dah!*" I shouted once she did, pulling out a brand-new, no-buttons-whatsoever, super-comfortable white J.Crew T-shirt from my dresser drawer and holding it up.

"Yay!" she cried, opening her eyes. Then she laughed out loud. "That is so *you,* Mom!"

She was right. Inside and out, I could honestly say, at least for now, that everything in my life was truly, profoundly, solidly, lovingly, and authentically *me.* And it felt wonderful.

Spring

Spring was slowly emerging and the gray haze that envelops Paris in winter was finally lifting. The city was bursting into color, and everything was coming alive.

Bright chartreuse leaves started peeking out from the branches of the trees along the boulevards and in the parks, and tulips were popping up in all the balcony window boxes atop the ornate bronze railings that typify Parisian buildings. Paris felt happy and hopeful, and so did I.

As I sat leisurely sipping a café au lait at Café Philosophe on rue de Temple in the Marais, watching the hip parade of cool people strolling by, I felt completely at ease in my own skin.

I was no longer the broken woman who ran to Paris, shattered into emotional smithereens and devoid of self-esteem after the collapse of my 32-year marriage. That version of me was nowhere to be found.

Feeling alive and endlessly enchanted by the world I was now a part of, I was overcome with gratitude to Paris for taking me in back then. This amazing city tough-loved me into bucking up and getting on with a much more beautiful and authentic version of my life and myself than the one I had been so deeply and insufferably committed to living before arriving here.

I was still figuring out the people, the culture, and the soul of Paris, but thankfully I was no longer also figuring out why I was so miserable inside. That feeling had gone as surely as the gray clouds of winter had disappeared.

Reflecting on the past two years, it felt as though my soul had enrolled in divine remedial school when moving here, sensing on the deepest level that it was time to learn some necessary lessons that, up until then, I had failed to grasp. And boy, what a steep learning curve it had been. In fact, my old self had completely unraveled and life here had reknitted an entirely new me.

One crazy apartment at a time, I've learned that I need solid and supportive ground under my feet. One beautiful tomato from the fresh market and baguette from the boulangerie at a time, I've learned to feed my soul. One face mask and moisturizer from the pharmacy at a time, I've learned to take care of my deepest needs. One café or bistro visit at a time, I've learned to slow down and enjoy the present moment. One washer-and-dryer load of clothing at a time, I've learned to be patient. One visit to the market at a time, I've learned to get out of my comfort zone and ask for help. One museum visit at a time, I've learned to broaden my interests and appreciate more than what is in my own head. And one stroll through this beautiful oasis at a time, I've learned to treasure the gift of life.

The greatest thing I've learned since moving here, however, is the healing power of letting go. I've had to let go of my anger and hurt. I've had to let go of my insecurities and financial fears. I've had to let go of my identity as a married person. And I've even had to let go of the way I think and speak, learning to communicate in a new language instead.

Being forced to let go of my old life, with all its unhappy attachments, as life demanded I do just a few short years ago, was a tremendous soul gift, as much as I hated to receive it. It brought me freedom.

I no longer overwork. I am no longer burdened by too many material things. I am no longer frustrated in my relationships. But most of all, I am no longer living in or making choices out of fear.

Fear still comes and goes, to be sure, but it doesn't camp out and hold my heart hostage any longer. Nor am I loyal to suffering as a noble cause as I once was. I love myself and my life and now know no one will love it more than I do. It is my responsibility to feel good, and it is my fault if I don't.

I still feel that I am a temporary visitor in Paris and often wonder what the hell I am doing here, but at the same time, I am now acutely aware that I am also a temporary visitor on this planet. Life is too short to waste on being committed to what is not authentically fulfilling while avoiding what could be. So mostly what I'm doing here is enjoying life fully.

Since moving here I have spoken with hundreds and hundreds of other women—clients and friends—who, having learned of my move to Paris, have shared how much they, too, wish they could leave their old lives behind and begin anew as well.

And I understand why. It sounds like such a dream. But I also know that as compelling as Paris itself is, their real yearning, and what I really came seeking when I moved here, is for a life that is rich, beautiful, soul satisfying, uplifting, and authentic instead of one that beats them down. That is what we all want in the end. I found my spiritual home in Paris; someone else might find it in Buenos Aires, Rome, Montreal, or Taos. Or maybe you're living there right now but just haven't opened your eyes to its inner beauty.

The endless challenge no matter where any of us lives is to choose what we take from all that our surroundings have to offer and put it together in a way that creates our own happiness. I am so glad I was willing to take it on. A person doesn't have to move to Paris to live an authentic life, and may not have to move at all. But we each do have to let go of what isn't working for us; face our deepest fears; ask for help; and be messy, vulnerable, and willing to give up being in control. We also have to pray a lot, trust that our spirit and intuition will guide us, believe that God will lead us, and accept that life will help us as we move forward into the unknown.

I am still learning all of this and more, but thankfully, now life's lessons aren't painful. They are exciting.

Just as I was finishing my coffee, my attention was drawn back to the moment. The local street artist I saw every time I visited that café came rambling down the street. He looked as if he were nearly 100 years old and dressed as a clown in ragged multicolored ribbed tights, a striped T-shirt, and a silly hat with bobbing balls dangling off the top. His bike was decorated with bells and whistles and horns and brightly painted nuts and bolts and other strange bits of hardware. A boom box on the handlebars played quintessentially French accordion music, and a group of Japanese tourists clamored after him to take a photo in exchange for a euro or two.

We exchanged glances and he winked at me in recognition. I smiled and waved. He was a walking billboard for living your dream, and I loved him for that.

I drank the last sip of coffee as I watched him pedal away after cashing in on the Japanese fans, then looked at my watch and realized I had to get going. I had an appointment in 20 minutes with an agent who was going to show me a brand-new apartment for rent in the 9th arrondisement, the chic yet bohemian area not far from Galleries Lafayette in the heart of the Right Bank of Paris, my new favorite part of town.

Yes, it was time to move again. I was ready for a new adventure and eager to see what lay ahead, and since in France a renter can break his or her lease at any time without penalty, I was free to explore.

While always open to an adventure, at least now I knew where my real home was.

Paris finally woke me up from the poison apple spell that lifetimes of self-rejection had put me under, causing me to desperately search for authentic love and belonging in all the wrong places.

With her unapologetically feminine antidote of truth removing all the confusion that led me astray, Paris graciously took me into her gorgeous bosom and sent me straight home, to the place of permanent love, where I had always belonged, in the center of my heart. And for this I am eternally grateful.

Acknowledgments

Waking Up In Paris, both as a book and on a personal level, came about with the loving support and help of so many people I cannot even begin to list and thank them all. But I will try.

The first person I want to acknowledge and thank with all my heart is Louise Hay, my beloved publisher, and the most inspirational woman I have ever been blessed to know.

Thank you for being my earth angel, my bold inspiration, my creative foundation, and now my angel in heaven. You understood, as a fellow Libra and lover of all that is beautiful, why I chose Paris. For you I am grateful every day.

I would also like to thank my longtime dear friend and fantastic editor Linda Kahn, who has been helping me write for more than 20 years. Linda, you are my guide, my teacher, and my believing eyes, and I thank you for sticking with me, and helping me tell my story, every step along the way. Without you I would be truly lost.

To my beloved daughter Sabrina Tully who courageously saved me from free-falling into despair and walked though this wall of fire alongside me, thank you for keeping me laughing, growing, and believing in what we were doing in Paris.

To my daughter Sonia, who was the voice of sanity and solid ground for both Sabrina and me when all seemed out of control and lost forever. Thank you for guiding us through the darkest nights with so much love and reassurance.

To Reid Tracy, my publisher, who has been a solid rock of support for more than 20 years. I am forever grateful for your continued belief in me and support in all ways. I am so blessed by your generosity.

I would also like to thank all my Hay House editors and friends. To my beloved friend and editor Patty Gift, who stood in the fire with me and kept the door open in Paris. Thank you for having my back all the way, and for the strength and encouragement you offered me at my lowest point. I love you forever.

To Sally Mason-Swaab, thank you for your masterful eye, and calm, grounded support in helping bring this book to life. And to your talented team behind the scenes who worked so hard to support this book and make it flow so beautifully. I am blessed beyond measure for your gifts and grace.

I'd like to deeply thank my dear friend Sam Horn for your loving coaching and honest feedback in helping me find my emerging self, my new path, and the best way to share my story, starting with our walk across the bridge in Maui. Your generous guidance and feedback have been invaluable in so many ways, and I'm so grateful.

I'd like to thank Carla Coulson for the amazing photo that we used for the book cover, and the creative fun and friendship between us that brought it about. You are so gifted and wonderful and I am grateful for all you are and do.

To Marion Ross, thank you for reminding me that life is a beautiful gift, and anything else is only temporary. You lift my heart and ground my emotions and keep me in the present.

I also want to thank Lu Ann Glatzmaier, my lifelong dear friend and soul mate, for your soul solace, your relentless wicked humor, and for assuring me that I am solidly on my path, no matter how confusing this particular passage in time might have been. And thank you for convincing me that croissants aren't fattening if made with love.

I'd like to thank my soul sister Wendy Lohr-Taylor. Your visits to Paris just to keep up my spirits up, month after month, over the past two years have been some of the best times I've had since moving here. Your friendship and encouragement were a beacon of light when it was all too easy to doubt everything.

To my sweet friend and soul brother Sandy Newbigging for that wonderful dinner together in London, where you suggested the title of this book. Thank you. It is perfect. I did wake up here.

I'd also like to thank Lilou Mace, Johannes (Butzi) Alhinac, David Brower, Veronique, Eric, Lynn Bell, Ralph Bilergi, and my angel Caspar for bringing Paris to life. I love you all. You make Paris the best place on earth to live.

And to the unseen forces of love and light in the Universe who have been my constant companions, guides, and friends in the subtle realms from the day I was born. This life has been such a great adventure and I draw the courage I've had to lean in and live full out from you, knowing I am never alone and always protected. Thank you from the depths of my soul.

About the Author

Sonia Choquette is celebrated worldwide as an author, spiritual teacher, six-sensory consultant, and transformational visionary guide. An enchanting storyteller, Sonia is known for her delightful humor and adept skill in quickly shifting people out of psychological and spiritual difficulties, and into a healthier energy flow. Because of her unique gifts, Sonia's expertise is sought throughout the world, helping both individuals and organizations dramatically improve their experience and abilities to perform at optimal levels through empowerment and transformation.

Sonia attended the University of Denver and the Sorbonne in Paris. She can be found sipping a café au lait or strolling along the streets somewhere in Paris today.

Website: www.soniachoquette.net

Hay House Titles of Related Interest

YOU CAN HEAL YOUR LIFE, the movie, starring Louise Hay & Friends
(available as a 1-DVD program, an expanded
2-DVD set, and an online streaming video)
Learn more at www.hayhouse.com/louise-movie

THE SHIFT, the movie,
starring Dr. Wayne W. Dyer
(available as a 1-DVD program, an expanded
2-DVD set, and an online streaming video)
Learn more at www.hayhouse.com/the-shift-movie

I CAN SEE CLEARLY NOW, by Dr. Wayne W. Dyer

*MARRIED TO BHUTAN: How One Woman Got
Lost, Said "I Do," and Found Bliss,* by Linda Leaming

*WALKING HOME: A Pilgrimage from
Humbled to Healed,* by Sonia Choquette

*YOU CAN HEAL YOUR HEART: Finding Peace After a
Breakup, Divorce, or Death,* by Louise Hay and David Kessler

All of the above are available at your local bookstore
or may be ordered by contacting Hay House (see next page).

We hope you enjoyed this Hay House book. If you'd like to receive our online catalog featuring additional information on Hay House books and products, or if you'd like to find out more about the Hay Foundation, please contact:

Hay House, Inc., P.O. Box 5100, Carlsbad, CA 92018-5100
(760) 431-7695 or (800) 654-5126
(760) 431-6948 (fax) or (800) 650-5115 (fax)
www.hayhouse.com® • www.hayfoundation.org

———

Published and distributed in Australia by:
Hay House Australia Pty. Ltd., 18/36 Ralph St., Alexandria NSW 2015
Phone: 612-9669-4299 • *Fax:* 612-9669-4144 • www.hayhouse.com.au

Published and distributed in the United Kingdom by:
Hay House UK, Ltd., Astley House, 33 Notting Hill Gate, London W11 3JQ
Phone: 44-20-3675-2450 • *Fax:* 44-20-3675-2451 • www.hayhouse.co.uk

Published in India by: Hay House Publishers India,
Muskaan Complex, Plot No. 3, B-2, Vasant Kunj, New Delhi 110 070
Phone: 91-11-4176-1620 • *Fax:* 91-11-4176-1630 • www.hayhouse.co.in

Distributed in Canada by:
Raincoast Books, 2440 Viking Way, Richmond, B.C. V6V 1N2
Phone: 1-800-663-5714 • *Fax:* 1-800-565-3770 • www.raincoast.com

———

Access New Knowledge.
Anytime. Anywhere.

Learn and evolve at your own pace
with the world's leading experts.

www.hayhouseU.com

Free e-newsletters
from Hay House, the Ultimate
Resource for Inspiration

Be the first to know about Hay House's free downloads, special offers, giveaways, contests, and more!

 Get exclusive excerpts from our latest releases and videos from *Hay House Present Moments*.

 Our *Digital Products Newsletter* is the perfect way to stay up-to-date on our latest discounted eBooks, featured mobile apps, and Live Online and On Demand events.

 Learn with real benefits! *HayHouseU.com* is your source for the most innovative online courses from the world's leading personal growth experts. Be the first to know about new online courses and to receive exclusive discounts.

 Enjoy uplifting personal stories, how-to articles, and healing advice, along with videos and empowering quotes, within *Heal Your Life*.

 Have an inspirational story to tell and a passion for writing? Sharpen your writing skills with insider tips from *Your Writing Life*.

Sign Up Now!

Get inspired, educate yourself, get a complimentary gift, and share the wisdom!

Visit www.hayhouse.com/newsletters to sign up today!